SALES
FOR NON-
SALESPEOPLE

ROBERT ASHTON

JOHN
MURRAY
LEARNING

First published in Great Britain in 2014 by John Murray Learning. An Hachette UK company.

First published in US in 2014 by The McGraw-Hill Companies, Inc.

This edition published 2015

British Library Cataloguing in Publication Data: a catalogue record for this title is available from the British Library.

Paperback ISBN 9781444795288

eBook ISBN 9781444795271

Library of Congress Catalog Card Number: on file.

1

The publisher has used its best endeavours to ensure that any website addresses referred to in this book are correct and active at the time of going to press. However, the publisher and the author have no responsibility for the websites and can make no guarantee that a site will remain live or that the content will remain relevant, decent or appropriate.

The publisher has made every effort to mark as such all words which it believes to be trademarks. The publisher should also like to make it clear that the presence of a word in the book, whether marked or unmarked, in no way affects its legal status as a trademark.

Every reasonable effort has been made by the publisher to trace the copyright holders of material in this book. Any errors or omissions should be notified in writing to the publisher, who will endeavour to rectify the situation for any reprints and future editions.

Typeset by Cenveo® Publisher Services.

Printed and bound in Great Britain by Clays Ltd, St Ives plc.

John Murray Learning policy is to use papers that are natural, renewable and recyclable products and made from wood grown in sustainable forests. The logging and manufacturing processes are expected to conform to the environmental regulations of the country of origin.

John Murray Learning

Carmelite House
50 Victoria Embankment

London EC4Y 0DZ

www.hodder.co.uk

Contents

INTRODUCTION

When I left college, my first job was with a multinational manufacturer of agricultural fertilizers. My job title was 'Technical Sales Representative' and my role to encourage farmers to buy my employer's products, rather than those of the competition. We used often complex technical arguments to encourage farmers to believe that, while our products were frequently costlier, they could give a greater financial return on investment than cheaper products.

Starting my career selling something that cost more meant that I had to learn how to do much more than simply offer the lowest price to win the orders. I had to persuade my customers that the additional benefits my product could give them more than compensated for the premium price. The problem, of course, was that farmers buy fertilizer to put on their growing crops. It might be six months before they see the additional yields I was promising – and then only if the weather had been kind to them.

Furthermore, this was 35 years ago. I had no laptop, mobile phone or Internet connection. I could not research my customers, or show them anything other than printed leaflets and fact sheets. Worse, I often struggled to find them as, once away from the farmyard, they could be contacted only by driving across the fields to where they were working.

The selling skills I learned all those years ago have helped me succeed in every one of the following years. That's not to say that I've always succeeded; but I have used those skills to encourage other people to hire me, promote me, take my ideas seriously and support the several new ventures I have started over the years.

As the world has changed, so, too, have my selling skills. It is no longer face-to-face verbal combat. Today, new connections are more often than not made online. Information (sometimes too much of it) is readily available and geography is no longer a barrier. With my iPad I can identify the people I need to influence, connect with them and even speak face to face using Skype, and all from the comfort of my living room, garden or favourite beach.

However, the process I follow – one I hope you will learn to follow, too – remains largely the same. It can be summarized by the mnemonic AIDA:

* **Attention** – you have to win the attention of the person you want to influence
* **Interest** – next you get them interested in what you have to offer
* **Desire** – then you help them see what's in it for them
* **Action** – finally, you need commitment.

Now, it's been many years since I considered myself a salesperson. My career roles have been far wider, although each has required me to influence the decision making of others. In fact, right at the beginning, my father was horrified to learn that my first job title contained the word 'sales'. To him – and perhaps to you, too – sales jobs come pretty low in the corporate pecking order.

So, while this book will be of huge benefit to anyone starting or developing a sales career, it is not written specifically with them in mind. The people for whom I've written this book are those who want to become more influential, to grow their career, see their ideas adopted and, yes, be good when faced with customers, too.

The simple fact is that none of us can succeed in life without winning the support of others. This book will help you do just that. Good luck!

PART I

Selling basics

1.

Attitude – why it's important to play to win

Let's go shopping

In my experience, as well as, I suspect, in yours, it's the staff you encounter in shops that make all the difference. I am as annoyed by those who pester me while I am browsing as I am by those who ignore me when I need assistance. Sometimes, however, someone gets it just right. They greet me, ask a few good questions and then help me make what feels like a good choice. In short, they sell to me professionally, politely and without pushing.

My bet is that you have had similar experiences. Truly exceptional salespeople are not loud, overbearing or intimidating. They are unobtrusive, show genuine interest and bend over backwards to make sure that you get exactly what you need. Of course, they'll also flatter you, but it's their honesty and enthusiasm that will win them your custom.

> 'I WAS THRILLED WHEN A DESIGNER SHOP ASSISTANT SAID
> I WAS A SIZE SMALLER THAN MADONNA!'
>
> ANNE ROBINSON

Is your porridge too hot?

You probably know the story of Goldilocks and the three bears. When she chanced upon their house and entered the kitchen, she found three bowls of porridge. One was too hot, one too cold and one just right. She ate every drop of the last one because she was hungry.

Now reflect on your recent shopping experiences. Try to group the salespeople you met as too hot, too cold or just right. I've listed some of my experiences in the table below. Are they similar to yours?

Too hot	• Grabbed me the moment I walked into the shop
	• Showed me products I wasn't interested in
	• Would not leave me alone
Too cold	• Ignored me, even when I'd been in the shop for ten minutes
	• Couldn't answer my questions about the product
	• Didn't take any interest in me at all
Just right	• Smiled at me when I walked in the shop
	• Took an interest in me and asked me what I wanted the product to do
	• Knew his/her stuff and recommended a product I'd not heard of, but proved to be just what I needed!

So now you know the selling basics. It's as simple as making an effort to find out what people want and then helping them to find it. If you work in a shop, it's your job to encourage people to buy what the business stocks. But not if that means the customer making a purchase they will quickly regret. Unhappy customers can quickly dent your reputation. It really is that straightforward.

! Get attitude

If you take a genuine interest in other people and try to understand their needs, you will find it easier to meet those needs to the benefit of you both.

Selling in a nutshell

The key differences between selling and ordinary conversations are that when selling you have:

• **a clear objective** – the commitment you want from the other person
• **control** – you gently direct the conversation in the direction you want it to go.

Of course, more often than not, when we speak with anyone we have an objective of sorts. It might just be to pass the time of day, or because you want to ask them something. For example:

• Could you please pass me another slice of cake?
• Can I take next Tuesday off as holiday, please?

If the answer is 'yes', you're fine – you have what you wanted. But if the answer is 'no', you might simply shrug your shoulders, say, 'Uh, OK then,' and accept being denied what you wanted. If you have some selling skills, you stand a chance of overcoming the problem of your request being refused.

You see, when people say 'no', they do not always mean 'no'. What they are really saying is that they don't yet see enough good reason for saying 'yes'. So let's take the examples a little further:

Could you please pass me another slice of cake?

No, you've had three already this afternoon.

But I'm training for a long run and need to eat lots – and your cake is very nice.

Oh, go on then – here you are.

Can I take next Tuesday off as holiday, please?

No, we've a large order to despatch that day and I need you in the warehouse helping out.

But I've been given tickets for a concert in Manchester and need to be there by 18:00.

Sorry, you should have asked me earlier; the answer's still no.

In the first example, explaining why you wanted a third slice of cake was enough to turn 'no' into 'yes'. But, in the second, the pressing workload meant that, even though you had a good reason for taking Tuesday off, the answer was still 'no'.

But you still want to take Tuesday off and so are faced with what appear to be three choices:

1 Miss the opportunity and go to work.
2 Call in sick, go to Manchester and hope that you don't get found out.
3 Keep trying to change your boss's mind.

Clearly, option 3 is best, so let's look at that a little closer.

Your boss believes she has a problem if you take Tuesday off. There's a large order to despatch and, although you work in the office, you and pretty much everyone else will be needed in the warehouse. Now think for a moment. The problem is not that you want the day off, but that your boss needs an extra pair of hands in the warehouse.

Now you have identified the real issue, you can solve it. Let's pick up the conversation:

> *Can I take next Tuesday off as holiday, please?*
>
> *No, we've a large order to despatch that day and I need you in the warehouse helping out.*
>
> *But I've been given tickets for a concert in Manchester and need to be there by 18:00.*
>
> *Sorry, you should have asked me earlier; the answer's still 'no'.*

Later on:

> *Boss, can I have another chat about taking Tuesday off, please – I have an idea!*
>
> *I'm really busy right now, but if you must; what is it?*
>
> *I called my nephew at lunchtime. He's home from college at the moment and looking for part-time work. He said he'd work for you for nothing on Tuesday and take my place in the warehouse. He hopes to impress you enough that you'll give him a few days' paid work when the warehouse is really busy and he's still in town.*
>
> *Well, thank you, I'd been thinking of getting a temp in, so let's give your nephew a try. Enjoy that concert!*

So by recognizing what the real need is and finding a solution, you get your way. That really is all that salespeople do. The clever bit is how they manage the conversation to identify exactly what is needed and how they can meet their needs.

It's all about technique and confidence. It's also about knowing what's possible and what's not. Finally, it's about being able to find sometimes hidden reasons for saying 'no'. Sometimes, finding the real reason for someone's reluctance to agree can be difficult. But we'll cover that later in the chapter.

Next I want to take you back to when you were very young. You see that you used some very useful sales techniques as a baby, but might have forgotten what they are. You see, selling is all about people and how they interact. There are techniques to help you focus on getting the result you want, and we will explore these in the later chapters in this section of the book. But, right now, I want to take you back to the basics of human communication.

Deepening your understanding of how and why we communicate will help you to influence the process. Then, when you add technique, you will do so with subtlety, and this will help you succeed.

Remember that this book is not just about selling products and services. I want to help you sell yourself, too, and become more influential in your life and work. The techniques are the same whatever you are selling.

Let's start by smiling

We all smile. In almost every culture around the world, when someone smiles, it means they're happy, welcoming and on your side. People have always smiled. It's how prehistoric people knew whether the people they'd met in the forest were friendly or likely to attack them.

Now we live in a very different world. It's been said that a city commuter encounters more people he or she doesn't know in an hour's journey than our prehistoric forebears did in a lifetime. For this reason, we no longer check out each person we meet with a smile; it would take too long.

But smiling remains the way we let people know that we're on their side. Smile at a stranger on the train, and chances are they'll smile back. Returning the smile acknowledges the fact that they no longer view you as a potential threat. If you're selling, that's very important!

To put it simply, if you're trying to influence someone, you'll be more successful and they'll be more at ease if you smile. It can be difficult to smile when you're concentrating on making an important point, but it will help if you can.

What's more, research has shown that we know instinctively whether a smile is sincere or put on for show. You see insincere smiles in restaurants sometimes; the head waiter greets you with a tired, artificial smile because it's become a habit. He's not really bothered about you as a person, just your ability to sit at a table and buy food. (Good waiters show genuine interest and are all the more popular as a result.)

'LET US ALWAYS MEET EACH OTHER WITH A SMILE, FOR THE SMILE IS THE BEGINNING OF LOVE.'

MOTHER TERESA

Speaking without words

Speech evolved a long time ago in the process of human evolution. It gives us a huge advantage over other species. But a surprising amount of our communication remains non-verbal. This is often called 'body language'.

We all read body language but often do not realize it. We subconsciously pick up on other people's posture, gestures and even tone of speech. We instinctively compare our interpretation of their body language with what they are saying. If the messages don't match, we become suspicious and distrustful.

Body language can be positive or negative. Here are some examples:

Positive body language	Negative body language
Smiling	Scowling
Standing tall	Slouching
Making eye contact	Avoiding eye contact
Speaking slowly and clearly	Speaking quickly
Open, gesturing arms	Folded arms

Influential people are usually very aware of their own body language. They try to avoid giving out negative signals and emphasize positive gestures. This helps them appear more credible, confident and reassuringly in control.

Politicians are taught how to use body language, particularly when appearing on TV. Try watching interviews on the TV news with the sound turned off. You'll be surprised by how easy it is to 'read' the people you can see, but cannot hear, speaking.

Getting your body language right is really important when you are selling because, when you meet people who don't know you, much of the impression they form will be from your body language. It's also important in your own workplace as your perceived attitude (positive or negative) will influence your popularity and success. Turn to Chapter 7 if you want to explore body language in more depth.

> 'NIXON IS A SHIFTY-EYED GODDAMN LIAR ... HE'S ONE OF THE FEW IN THE HISTORY OF THIS COUNTRY TO RUN FOR HIGH OFFICE TALKING OUT OF BOTH SIDES OF HIS MOUTH AT THE SAME TIME AND LYING OUT OF BOTH SIDES.'
>
> HARRY S. TRUMAN

! Get attitude

Stand tall and look people in the eye, even if they are taller than you.

Being positive

Norman Vincent Peale's book *The Power of Positive Thinking* has been continuously in print for more than 60 years. It's a book that encourages self-belief and, it could be argued, spawned the very popular self-help genre of books. The fact is that everyone wants to be positive, yet many find it difficult. We just all enjoy a good moan that little bit too much.

To be successful, you have to believe in what you are doing. If you do not, you will come across as somehow insincere. No amount of smart talking or managed body language will overcome that. The simple fact is that, if you believe it's good, others will be more likely to agree when you tell them.

Successful people believe in themselves. They have the resilience to bounce back from knocks, and always seem upbeat. Of course, they will have moments of doubt, but they keep these private. A good recent example of someone with boundless self-belief is the British politician Boris Johnson, currently London's mayor. Johnson manages to capture people's imagination and make the seemingly impossible seem achievable. He also has the knack of turning negative events into positive press coverage. He looks on the bright side and encourages others to do the same.

Here are three things you can easily do to become more positive:

1 **Set realistic goals** – if you know what success looks like to you, it will be far easier to achieve it. What's more, coping with the inevitable

difficulties that you certainly will meet along the journey will be easier, because you know that it's all getting you closer to your goal. We will cover goal setting fully in Chapter 6.

2 **Keep things in perspective** – always view the setbacks within the context of the bigger picture. For example, just because you didn't get the promotion job you wanted, you remain a top-performing, respected member of the team. Your current job pays the bills and there will be other opportunities to climb the career ladder. However, if you become bitter and resentful, you will limit your future options. Negative people rarely get promoted.

3 **Keep the company of positive people** – it's so easy to feel sorry for people who always seem to be down on their luck. Negative people tend to have negative experiences and, worse, can pull you down to their level of despair. Try to spend time with people who see opportunities rather than threats.

> 'ALWAYS LOOK ON THE BRIGHT SIDE OF LIFE.'
>
> ERIC IDLE (MONTY PYTHON SONG LYRIC)

! **Get attitude**

Believe in yourself, know where you want to go and be confident that you will one day arrive.

Give and take

Perhaps the single biggest reason why people buy anything is that they can clearly see something in it for them. This might sound obvious, and indeed in some situations it is. For example, if you're out for the day and feel hungry, you might buy a sandwich. You know that the sandwich will stop you feeling hungry and so, if you have the money in your pocket, you'll likely as not pop into the next shop you see and buy one.

The situation becomes less clear when you are presented with a choice. Perhaps you find a sandwich shop and next door is a shop selling hot pies. It's cold outside and, although you set out to buy a sandwich, the pie shop wins your order. Both of these decisions are made without talking to either shopkeeper.

Once you enter either shop, it's the job of the person behind the counter to make it as easy as possible for you to buy something. You want to eat and they want to sell you food. But here your respective priorities start to diverge. You just want something to eat; they want to sell you as much as they can persuade you to carry out of the shop.

Furthermore, you don't want to eat too much, as feeling stuffed is actually more uncomfortable than feeling hungry. Let's look at some options facing the shop assistant:

- You ask for a sandwich and they offer you a free drink if you buy two. That means that they sell more, but you feel too full. They will gain more than you from the transaction so you say 'no'.
- You ask for a sandwich and they ask whether you'd like a drink as well. You say 'yes', that's a good idea. Then they suggest a chocolate bar for later. 'Hmm,' you think, 'Yes, I'll be late home tonight so that's a good idea.' Now you have bought more than you intended and the shop assistant has helped you avoid feeling hungry again before you get home.

In the first example, it's all about selling and how the customer feels is not really considered. In the second, the shop assistant is actually being helpful and encouraging you to stock up on food for later in the day. They're being thoughtful and considerate; they're also talking you into selling more.

In every single situation where you are trying to sell anyone anything, you will succeed only if the other person can see clearly that they will benefit as much, if not more, from the transaction than you. For example:

- People get promoted at work because they've shown how they will become more useful (profitable) to their employer than the extra cost of the pay rise.
- Your project will win the go-ahead over someone else's because you've convinced people that the return on investment will be greater or the chances of failure lower.
- Your hotel's Trip Advisor reputation for attentive service will be more influential in winning you bookings than a heavily discounted price.

'SURE I'M FOR HELPING THE ELDERLY. I'M GOING TO BE OLD MYSELF SOME DAY.'

LILLIAN CARTER (MOTHER OF US PRESIDENT JIMMY CARTER)

! Get attitude

If you always put your customer's needs before your own, you'll find yourself selling far more than you expected.

In this chapter you've discovered:

- that good salespeople are not too pushy, nor do they ignore you
- that selling is about making life easier for other people in ways that benefit you both
- that, if you're confident and self-assured, others will find you more convincing.

2.

Benefits – understanding what makes people say 'yes'

Let's start by being honest

We all put ourselves first. It's the way humans are made. If you're a parent, you'll know that babies can be very demanding. They can quite literally scream for attention and, certainly to start with, never say thank you. Deep down, we remain that self-centred throughout our lives.

As we grow up, we learn that giving something in return makes it more likely that our demands will be met. In fact, most of us were taught to express gratitude because it is polite to do so. 'Give Granny a kiss to say thank you for your present' is the kind of thing mothers say, or at least mine did when I was small. You quickly learn that kissing Granny leads to more treats than giving her the cold shoulder.

This is where we learn our early sales behaviour. To put it simply, grannies will be more generous if they are rewarded for the gifts and treats they give their grandchildren. And they do this because there's something in it for them, even if it's only the fleeting perception of being deeply loved.

Benefits, then, are what's in it for us – in other words, the benefit we will derive from the transaction. We buy a drink on a train because it will quench our thirst. We kiss our granny because she then gives us more presents. Probably, without that incentive, we'd not kiss her that often at all.

'I'M SELFISH, IMPATIENT, AND A LITTLE INSECURE.'

MARILYN MONROE

Features and benefits

Imagine for a moment that you are preparing for a job interview. You are hoping to sell your prospective new employer the idea that you're the perfect person for the job. You have already supplied a CV listing your skills and experience. Referees are also lined up to endorse your application. You dress to impress, but whether or not you are successful will be dictated by how well you demonstrate that you can do the job.

The interview panel will hire you if they are convinced that you can deliver what is demanded by the job. That is the benefit they will gain by taking you on. You may bring additional benefits they consider desirable, rather than essential – for example, fluency in a second language. It is these benefits they will be buying.

But you are you – a person with skills, experience, knowledge and personality. These are what we call 'features'. They are things you have that might be of some benefits to a new boss. Features alone will not win you the job; it's how they translate into *benefits* that matters. In fact, features you particularly prize might be of no value to your employer at all. Perhaps you can drive a lorry but are applying for an office job.

An important lesson we all have to learn is that it's only really worth talking about the features that are going to benefit the buyer. The trouble is that often we want to talk about what we're most proud of; however, if that's not of interest to our customer, you will quickly lose their interest. So:

• features are what something *has*

• benefits are what something *does*.

For example:

• Feature – the golf ball is red

• Benefit – red golf balls are easier to find in long grass (of greatest value to novice golfers who slice their shots and so spend a lot of time searching for their balls in long grass).

Clearly, not everyone is the same and you will find out whether Janet is a better golfer than Justin only if you ask the right questions. What's more, you need to ask them sensitively; Justin might not readily admit to being a poor golfer.

Here is another example:

• Edward buys logs for his wood-burning stove because he is a passionate environmentalist and wants to reduce his carbon footprint.

• Jessica buys logs for her stove because she has no mains gas and finds heating oil expensive.

• Christopher is planning a romantic evening with his girlfriend and plans to seduce her in front of a blazing log fire.

Each person is in the market for some logs, but each for a very different reason:

- Edward is more interested in the sustainability of the woodland than the price of the logs, but he's no fool and doesn't want to waste money.
- Jessica buys logs to save money and so is really only interested in the price.
- Christopher will pay the highest price of all, but only wants to buy enough logs for one evening.

Now imagine that you are selling logs. What will you tell each of our three customers and what will you sell them?

Here's how it might work:

- Edward was interested in the history of your woodland and decided to visit and collect his logs himself. He bought a car load which you put into bags. He paid £100 for the logs because you took off the delivery charge, then added on something for the bags. He didn't want to get his car dirty.
- Jessica wanted cheap logs that were small enough for her wood-burner. She paid £100 because you delivered them and stacked them in her porch, making it easier for her to carry them in.
- Christopher ordered from your website, so didn't really talk to you at all. He wanted a small bag of logs, around 10 per cent of the amount the other two bought. But he added kindling and a box of firelighters to his order, as well as ticking the box for rosewood which your website described as having a sweet scent. He paid £50 and you delivered his logs on your way to Jessica's house.

Can you see how, while each purchased from the same pile of logs in the depot, the benefits sought were quite different. Moreover, these different benefit expectations meant that each was willing to pay a different price.

> ## ! See benefits
>
> People buy benefits not features. It's not what it is but what it does for me that I'm prepared to pay for.

Quantifiable benefits

Helping someone recognize the benefits of what you are suggesting is only half the battle. They have to become sufficiently motivated to do something as a result. If you're selling in a shop, they have to be confident enough to make a purchase, rather than walk out and buy nothing. You want them to say 'yes' right now.

If you've just been interviewed for a new job, you've described the benefits of hiring you over other candidates, but it's unlikely that you were offered the job on the spot. Somehow, the interviewer has to remember all the pertinent points for when the decision is actually made, perhaps a day or two later.

To do this, you need to quantify the benefits and compare them with the cost. The more the benefits to the buyer outweigh the cost, the more appealing the decision to buy becomes.

For example:

- A combined desk top copier, scanner and printer costs £300.
- A similar printer without the additional features costs £200, as does a copier/scanner.
- So you pay £100 more for the additional features of the combined machine and save the additional £100 you'd spend to buy the machines separately. However, the additional investment is only worth while if you need to scan and copy things.

It's the job of the salesperson in the shop to help you decide. They ask you how often you need to copy or scan documents. More importantly, they ask you how you do that right now, even if only now and again. Perhaps you pop out to the library and use a copier there.

'How long does it take to go to the library to run off a couple of copies?' they ask you. 'And how pleasant is that journey if it's a cold, wet, dark winter's afternoon?' Most of us would quickly see the convenience of the combined machine, even if it just meant avoiding the occasional, inconvenient run into town.

It might also be possible to put a value on that convenience – to quantify it in a way that makes the additional cost appear great value. For example:

How often do you need to copy or scan? – Perhaps once a week.

How do you travel to the library to do that? – On the bus.

What's the fare? – £2 return.

So after 50 trips, you've covered the additional cost of the combined machine. – Well, yes!

Well, the machine has a two-year warranty, over which time it will save you £200 in bus fares; it's actually making you money! – Put like that, I guess you're right.

And how long does it take to make the round trip? – Hmm, sometimes an hour if I miss a bus.

And what could you do with that extra hour a week? – Well, I could take a long hot bath and relax; life does get pretty hectic.

Can you see how the conversation has led to the combined printer/copier offering two very appealing benefits? A cost saving that you can quantify and something self-indulgent you can do with the time you save.

Both are important. It is probably the cost saving you will use to justify the purchase in your mind. But what really tips the balance is the thought of a long relaxing bath; something you rarely have time to enjoy. You walk out of the shop carrying the combined printer/copier.

Now, in reality, you probably don't just go into town to copy some papers in the library. You might have other errands to run, or meet a friend for coffee. But the salesperson isolated the relevant activities in your mind, and then helped you justify the price premium of the combined machine. That's called selling!

'TIME IS MONEY.'

BENJAMIN FRANKLIN

Tangible and intangible benefits

In the previous example, there were two benefits to buying the combined machine: one a cost saving in bus fares, the other the opportunity for a nice long soak once a week. One of the paradoxes of selling is that, more often than not, the bath is a more influential benefit than the cost saving.

That's because one appeals to us *emotionally* and the other *logically*. Most of the time, we use our emotions to make decisions, then justify them using logic. The most effective salespeople help you see both the emotional and logical appeal of the product or service they want you to buy.

The logical, more obvious benefits you can quantify are called 'tangible benefits'. The emotional, harder-to-quantify ones are called 'intangible benefits'. Most decisions we make are because we can see (or have been shown) both tangible and intangible benefits. For example:

- Both James and Jane have very similar qualifications and experience and both could do the job. However, I think Jane will fit in better because she clearly has a great sense of humour.

- We have £10,000 and can invest in only one development project. Both Julian's new widget and Jon's new customer care programme will deliver similar results. But Jon's programme will, I think, improve our market reputation so he wins the budget.

- Both the Honda and Nissan are excellent cars and both are British made. But the top-of-the-range Nissan comes with a lot more gadgets and so I've ordered that one.

Clearly, the ratio of tangible to intangible benefits will vary depending on what it is you are buying. But, in every single situation, there will be both. For example:

- College A won the corporate training contract, even though College B had more experience of the sector and both were similarly priced. The reason? Because College A had a smart new building where they met the corporate HR team and gave them a nice lunch.

- I love listening to Dire Straits (it's my age, I know) but use logic to choose between buying a CD, a download or simply streaming the music via my Spotify subscription.

- Premier Inn is just one of a number of budget hotel chains in the UK. But they are the only one to offer a money back guarantee if you don't get a good night's sleep. Making the offer suggests they are confident I will sleep well there and so they get my business.

In each case, it is the intangible benefits that clinch the deal. A nice lunch provides an opportunity to get to know the people who hope to supply you with training. We buy music CDs and downloads, even though it's cheaper to stream. The promise of a good night's sleep will encourage us to drive just that little bit out of our way to stay in a Premier Inn, rather than a similarly priced hotel that makes no promises.

> **! See benefits**
>
> We will pay more for things that make us feel good than we will for things that simply
> save us money.

'I JUST WANT TO BE ABLE TO PLAY AND MAKE PEOPLE FEEL GOOD WITH WHAT I DO. WHEN
YOU'RE THINKING THAT WAY, ANYTHING CAN HAPPEN.'

MARK KNOPFLER

Sticky benefits

Not every decision is made while you are present. Other options often
have to be explored before an order is placed or a successful candidate is
offered the job. So not only do you have to quantify the benefits you are
offering, you have to make them memorable. In other words, you have to
make them *sticky*.

Sticky benefits are those that:

• have strong emotional appeal and are likely to be remembered

• create desire and ambition, so people will save up if they can't yet afford
the cost

• get talked about, creating additional demand.

In fact, it could be argued that promotional marketing is also about
creating sticky benefits. Because the marketer never meets their
prospective customers face to face, the benefits they promote have to be
accurately targeted at the right audience. This is something we will explore
in Chapters 6 and 17.

There are three techniques marketers use to make benefits stick that are
useful right now:

1 **Scarcity** – there are only so many and when they're gone, they're gone (e.g.
discounted stock of the current car model when a new one is launched).

2 **Urgency** – order today because rising material costs mean the price
goes up next week (e.g. energy companies and mortgage lenders use
this to sell long-term contracts).

3 **Fashion** – everyone else has already got one; you don't want to be left out (e.g. mobile phones where differences between new and old models are marginal).

Just suppose that you identify in a job interview a skill you have that will make life a lot easier for your prospective new manager. It won't necessarily benefit the organization. Perhaps you're really good with Twitter and the manager needs help building their own profile. Make sure that an offer to help them master Twitter is made right at the end of the interview. If they have a Twitter account, but hardly use it, ask for the @address and follow them immediately. You won't need to do more and you will be remembered.

When selling a product or service, you make it sticky using storytelling. But, unlike conventional storytelling, where you tell the story, you encourage your prospective customer to do so. You do this by asking them to describe how they will feel. This will create an emotional connection that will linger long after you have parted.

It's one of the reasons test-driving new cars is such an important part of the selling process. Of course you want to know how the car drives, but the salesperson will go to great lengths to make sure you become comfortable with the car, too. In short, the more you imagine what it would be like to own the car, the more likely you are to buy it.

> **! See benefits**
>
> The better our memory of something, the more likely we are to return to it later.

In this chapter you've discovered:

- that people buy because of how they will benefit personally by doing so
- that quantifying (costing) the benefit makes it easier to justify the price
- that people use emotion to make buying decisions then use logic to justify them.

3.
Questions – how to lead a conversation where you want it to go

All about questions

We all ask questions. It's how we get other people to help or share information with us. Put simply, a question is a request. Questions demand answers, and in most societies it is considered impolite to ignore and not answer a question. Selling is all about asking questions. More specifically, selling is about asking questions in a way that directs the conversation and leads to an agreement.

In fact, to ignore a question can make us feel quite uncomfortable. People will often say they have been 'put on the spot' by a difficult question. Politicians are good at avoiding difficult questions; it's something they quickly learn to do. But most of us will quickly be embarrassed if asked a question we'd really rather not answer.

So, when you're selling, it's important to strike a balance between pushing too hard and not directing the conversation at all. Push too hard and you risk alienating the other person. But, if there's no apparent direction to the conversation, the other person will quickly lose interest, especially if you have interrupted them when they were busy.

Professional salespeople are usually very mindful of time. That's because the more people they talk to, the more sales they are likely to make. They are encouraged to establish rapport and then quickly get to the point. When it becomes obvious they have a sale, they will summarize, ask for the order, confirm the deal and move on. There's no point in continuing the conversation once you have a 'yes'. It just provides opportunity for doubts to creep into your customer's mind.

This might sound quite manipulative and cold, but the skill is in the way you lead the conversation. You use questions to manage both speed and direction. That way, everyone feels relaxed and decisions get made.

'MY METHOD IS TO TAKE THE UTMOST TROUBLE TO FIND THE RIGHT THING TO SAY, AND THEN TO SAY IT WITH THE UTMOST LEVITY'

GEORGE BERNARD SHAW

Listening

There's a lot of truth in the well-known adage that says we have two ears and one mouth and should use them in that proportion. After all, there's nothing worse than telling someone something only to realize they've not been listening.

Successful selling is as much about listening as it is speaking. Before we explore the different questioning techniques, it's important to reflect on the importance of effective listening. This means much more than just allowing the other person to speak and hearing what they say. It means clearly making the effort to understand their message.

Let me make a confession. I find listening incredibly difficult. I often quickly work out where the other person is heading and have an almost compulsive urge to interrupt, finish their point for them and then add my own. This, of course, can appear rude and undermines their confidence. Worst of all, I'm not always right. It's always better to hear someone out than assume that you know what's coming next.

Here are some simple ways you can improve your listening:

- Make time for the conversation – if you don't have time, don't start the conversation.
- Avoid distraction and concentrate on what is being said – for example, don't check your emails while talking on the phone.
- Watch the speaker's body language and think beyond the words they're using to interpret how they feel about what they're saying.
- Don't let your own views cloud your interpretation of what is being said to you – you can only influence when you've taken the trouble to really understand.
- Never, ever interrupt and don't start speaking the moment they stop.

As well as listening more effectively, it's important to demonstrate to the other person that you are listening and understanding what they're saying. You can do this by maintaining eye contact, smiling and nodding in agreement (or frowning if unsure). Professional salespeople also make a point of reflecting back key words or phrases in their reply; sometimes, just repeating one word will keep them talking. For example:

Tell me more about your dog.

*Well, he's a spaniel. He's full of energy and loves going into **the sea**.*

The sea?

*Yes, whenever we go for a walk on the beach, he's always launching himself into the sea – even in the middle of winter when it's really **cold**.*

*Doesn't he feel the **cold** then?*

*I guess not – he just runs and runs when he comes out and I guess that keeps him **warm**.*

I've made the key words bold to show you how they have been repeated. Salespeople reflect the words that matter most. It enables them to direct the conversation using very few words. Remember that everyone enjoys a conversation more when they're doing most of the talking!

Finally, it's almost inevitable that, as you work on improving your questioning, you will find listening more difficult. The temptation is to half listen and, at the same time, work out what your next question will be. The best way to avoid this is to take your time. It's OK to pause and leave time to think before responding with your next question.

'I LIKE TO LISTEN. I HAVE LEARNED A GREAT DEAL FROM LISTENING CAREFULLY. MOST PEOPLE NEVER LISTEN.'

ERNEST HEMINGWAY

! **Think questions**

You can only ask a good next question if you've listened to the answers to those you asked earlier.

Open and closed questions

There are two kinds of questions that we all use every day of our lives. They are called open questions and closed questions.

Open questions encourage someone to share information or an opinion, for example:

• What did you think of the football last night?
• How do you feel the new job is going?

Closed questions seek confirmation or agreement, for example:

• Would you like the green one or the blue one?
• Are you enjoying the new job?

Can you see how similar the two second examples are? If I ask you the question 'How do feel the new job is going?', you have the opportunity to express an opinion and perhaps support that with some examples. You might say something like: 'Well, it's OK, but not quite what I expected as I'm spending a lot more time doing paperwork than I was led to believe.'

The second question, 'Are you enjoying the new job?', can really only be answered with a 'yes' or 'no' – although, to be fair, you can then go on to say: 'No, because I have to do more paperwork than I was led to believe.'

So, to control a conversation, you use both open questions and closed questions: open to find stuff out and closed to check that you have understood and to gain commitment. Here's an example. I've marked with an (o) or a (c) which are open and which are closed questions:

(o) *Good morning, how are you today?*

Fine, thank you.

(o) *What would you like this morning?*

A cappuccino, please.

(c) *Would you like chocolate or cinnamon on top?*

Chocolate.

(o) *What about something to eat?*

No, I don't think so, not today.

(c) *We've got some really nice, small croissants in today. They're just a pound and selling really well. Would you like one with your coffee?*

Erm, yes, why not? Thank you.

In this example, we use open questions:

- to break the ice and start the conversation
- to ask what the customer would like
- having taken the coffee order, to see whether the customer would like to eat as well (because not to ask would deny you the opportunity to increase the value of the order).

Can you see how the conversation naturally uses both open and closed questions? This example also introduces one of the most important principles of selling. That is that 'no' does not always mean 'no'. The clue was the word 'think' in the answer 'No, I don't think so, not today.' It was not a decisive 'No thank you' but hinted at uncertainty or indecision.

! Think questions

'No' does not always mean 'no'. It often means 'I've not yet decided.'

We'll cover open and closed questions again in Chapters 4, 13 and 16 where you'll have the chance to try using them in different situations.

Leading questions

A leading question is rather like a beam of light, highlighting the way you want the conversation to go. When you ask a leading question, you make an assumption. You assume that the conversation will go in a certain direction and make a start. The person you are talking to has to either follow or challenge. Leading questioning can be powerful; it can also be very annoying, making you feel that you are being pushed somewhere you might not want to go.

Leading questions also help you clarify specific points about which you might have doubts – for example 'How soon would you like them delivered?' The question forces the other person either to suggest a date or to explain what other option they have in mind.

Salespeople use leading questions to speed up conversations and encourage people gently towards making a decision. Remember that often several decisions will need to be made before a sale is made. We'll cover this process in the next chapter.

Leading questions can be open or closed. For example:

- **Open** – 'Tell me about your hobbies?'
- **Open leading** – 'Tell me about your stamp collection?' (You are focusing on just one hobby.)
- **Closed** – 'Do you ever sell stamps from your collection?'
- **Closed leading** – 'Would you sell me that duplicate Penny Black you mentioned that you had?'

Leading questions often start with what, when, where, why, who, which or how. Right now, knowing when to ask which type of question probably feels a little daunting. Don't worry, because as you read through the book you'll see plenty of examples of how all the different kinds of question can be used.

! **Think questions**

Remember that you already have a lifetime's experience of asking good questions. Understanding questions better will help you ask them more effectively.

Finding feelings

You've already read that we use emotion to make a decision and then logic to justify it to ourselves and others. This will probably be more true if you're buying a holiday than a loaf of bread. That said, you might feel that an organic loaf is better for you and so worth the higher price.

The key word here is *feel*. We do what we feel is going to be best, right or most appropriate given the choices we are faced with. So to help someone reach the right decision for them – and, of course, you – it's important to know how they feel about things.

The way to find out is to use feelings words in your question. So rather than asking, 'What do you like most about the kitchen?', you could ask, 'What do you love most about the kitchen?' Using the word 'love' will inevitably prompt an answer that reveals more about how the person feels.

Equally, you can use feelings words to discover what people like least about something. So, if you were selling car breakdown insurance, you could ask, 'What worries you most about breaking down?' or, 'What do you fear most about breaking down?' Fear is another feelings word. We feel fear, but do not feel worry. Worrying is usually the product of a fear.

Here are some more words you might use:

Emotional	Logical
Love	Like
Fear	Worry
Hate	Dislike
Enjoy	Prefer
Want	Need

Reflect on recent conversations you've had. Did you use emotional or logical words? Often, the more confident you are, the more likely that you will use emotional words in your everyday conversation. If you do, others will be inclined to consider you warmer, more caring. Selling is all about making people feel happier.

'WHEN DEALING WITH PEOPLE, REMEMBER YOU ARE NOT DEALING WITH CREATURES
OF LOGIC, BUT CREATURES OF EMOTION.'

DALE CARNEGIE

! Think questions

The feeling of success is emotional. So using emotional language will make you appear, and become, more successful.

Ice-breakers

Let's end this chapter by looking at ice-breakers. These are the questions you ask to engage someone you don't know in conversation. This is very different from meeting someone you know, when you'll start by greeting each another and the conversation starts naturally; you won't have to think about it. Strangers are different and somehow always appear unapproachable.

A shop is a good place to look at ice-breakers first. It's where most of us have been accosted by someone we don't know, trying to sell us something. Typically, they will make eye contact and ask, 'How can I help you?' This, as you now know, is an open question. It is also easily deflected with 'Thanks, but I'm happy just browsing.'

A better ice-breaker in a shop would be 'What brought you in here today?' or, 'What can I help you with today?' Both are open questions, but a little more focused. An ice-breaker question needs to be one you can easily ask, but not one that you use every time. Overuse makes it almost impossible to deliver with meaning and sincerity. Which is why we all hate it when someone in a shop asks, 'How can I help you?' You can tell they don't really care what the answer's going to be.

But just suppose that you are at an event and want to engage someone in conversation. Perhaps it's even worse: you're at a business networking event and everyone else seems to be deep in conversation. You're on your own. It's one of the most daunting situations you can encounter at work.

Here are five ice-breaker questions you can adapt and use:

- 'May I join you?' is direct and to the point. It almost always means a group of people will let you join the group and include you in their conversation.
- 'What did you think of the last presentation/lunch/news that...?' The more relevant the question to something you've both witnessed or experienced, the easier things will be.
- 'I love that skirt – may I ask where you bought it?' Flattery can get you a long, long way.
- 'What do you think about ... [whatever it is the person is looking at]?'

- 'I always find it difficult to start conversations at networking events. Do you?' is almost guaranteed to make you a new friend if you ask someone who's on their own and looking lost.

A good way to practise conversation, and in particular your questioning techniques, is to talk to strangers. I do it all the time, especially on trains or in other situations where circumstances put strangers together. You'll be surprised by how quickly you become more confident at this. You'll also be fascinated by what you discover about people. Under the surface, we're all pretty much the same.

'THERE ARE NO STRANGERS HERE; ONLY FRIENDS YOU HAVEN'T YET MET.'

W.B. YEATS

In this chapter you've discovered:

- that you can steer a conversation by asking open and closed questions
- that listening to what people say is more important than the questions you ask them
- that asking what people love or fear will be more revealing than asking what they like or dislike.

4.
Process – the sales conversation, step by step

Helping people make the right decisions

It may seem obvious, but people buy things because they want them. Or at least they think they do at the moment the decision is made. We've all bought things on impulse and regretted it later. It could be as simple as eating a second slice of cake and then feeling sick. Or hiring someone because you like them, when deep down you know they're wrong for the job.

Perhaps worse is letting your head rule your heart and not buying something when you have only a fleeting opportunity to do so. I still occasionally regret not buying a pocket knife that particularly caught my eye when visiting Canada. The fact that I had just that one opportunity to buy it means that, however much I regret making the wrong decision, I cannot reverse it.

As you've already discovered, the decision to purchase anything is emotionally driven. That makes it hard for the buyer to be objective, yet objectivity is needed to justify the decision, if only to themselves. So the role of a salesperson is to help others make what for them is the right decision at the right time. It's not about pushing people into making a decision that's only right for the salesperson. Today, more perhaps than ever before, selling is about helping people make *good* decisions.

The way you do this is by following a clear, logical sales process. You use good questioning technique to help your customer recognize, and ideally quantify, the benefits to them of making the purchase.

> **! Understand selling**
>
> Good selling is helping people make good decisions.

Why people buy

Before we look at the sales process, here's a really useful mnemonic that can help you focus on what matters most. Believe it or not, there are only six reasons why people say 'yes'. I call them 'buying motives'. The more of these you can meet, the greater the likelihood you'll get your sale. The mnemonic is SPACED:

- **Safety** – Is it safe? Will it conflict with what I already have or use?
- **Performance** – What does it actually do? Will it deliver what is promised?
- **Appearance** – Does it look good and, moreover, will having it make me look good?
- **Convenience** – Is it simple? Can I take one away with me today?
- **Economy** – Does it represent value for money? Are the running costs low or crippling?
- **Durability** – Will it last or wear out? How long before it becomes out of date and superseded by something better?

These apply equally to any decision you are trying to influence, at home as well as at work. Your partner, mother or kids are more likely to act on your suggestions if you show them how they meet their SPACED needs.

> 'OUR PRIME PURPOSE IN THIS LIFE IS TO HELP OTHERS. AND IF YOU CAN'T HELP THEM, AT LEAST DON'T HURT THEM.'
>
> DALAI LAMA

How to sell

There are four steps to the selling process, summarized by the mnemonic AIDA:

- **Attention** – You have to win the attention of the person you want to influence.
- **Interest** – Next you get them interested in what you have to offer.
- **Desire** – Then you help them see what's in it for them.
- **Action** – Finally, you need commitment.

A good salesperson will steer the encounter through each of these steps, in sequence, seamlessly slipping from one to the next. When the final 'action' stage is reached and commitment sought, the answer will often initially be 'no'.

This is called an 'objection'. It's the reason given for not agreeing to the deal. You overcome the objection by asking more questions to better understand the problem. Then, having resolved the objection, you ask once more for commitment.

So the AIDA sequence is not strictly linear. You can, and will, loop back from time to time. In fact, often the best way to sell is to seek commitment often and early. The objections will help you focus your presentation on the features and benefits that are of greatest interest. There's little more boring than being told all about something that doesn't interest you.

Let's look at the principles of each step in more detail. Later, as you work through the other parts of this book, you'll come across AIDA again.

Attracting attention

My first job was selling to farmers. This was before we had mobile phones and so, unless you were lucky and they were in the farmhouse, you had to drive across the fields to find where they were working. They would stop the tractor, open the door, look down at me standing in the field and ask me what I wanted. They rarely liked being disturbed.

This was not an ideal way to attract attention. For one thing, it was time-consuming for me, as farmers can be hard to find when out working their land. But worse was the fact I had interrupted them without warning and forced them to stop what they were doing.

What's more I was young and naive, so I would launch into my current campaign pitch without bothering to ask them even how they were. Not only did I interrupt them; I failed to give them a good reason for doing so.

Attracting someone's attention physically is only one part of the challenge. You have to show genuine interest in them and their situation quickly. In other words, you have to get on the same wavelength and show genuine interest in them and their current situation. For example, you walk into your boss's office just as she shouts 'I hate you' and slams the phone down. You're there for a prearranged meeting to discuss a new project. You could:

- ignore the outburst and talk about your project proposal
- ask whether she's OK and discuss the project once she's calmed down.

Clearly, the second option will probably work better. By sympathizing with her anger and asking whether she's OK you have shown some empathy with her situation. She might even suggest you give her some time and return later. This might be inconvenient but actually gives you an advantage. By putting you out, she will feel slightly more obliged to support the project you want to discuss with her. In short, you have established rapport.

Rapport is that comfortable feeling that the person you are with is in tune with you. Once rapport is established, there's automatically a degree of trust and interest. Professional salespeople appear naturally affable and friendly. They will:

- ask you how you feel today and listen to your answer
- nod or smile when appropriate to show you're holding their interest
- keep eye contact with you, but not stare and make you feel uncomfortable
- reflect back key words or phrases to encourage you to talk.

Once you have the full attention of your prospective customer and have established some rapport, you can move on to stimulating their interest.

Good attention-grabbing questions might include:

- 'I see you're looking at our range of printers. What do you most want your new printer to be able to do?'
- 'Excuse me; you look the kind of person who'd be willing to give me two minutes to hear why I'm raising money to beat cancer.'
- 'I chanced upon your LinkedIn profile and would really like to hear how you are finding the green-energy marketplace right now.'

Developing interest

The more interested someone becomes in what you are selling, the more likely they are to buy it. The salesperson's job then is to develop interest until it tips into desire. You do this by asking questions to identify, then quantify, the benefits your customer will gain from the product or service you are selling.

There are, however, two starting points for the salesperson needing to develop someone's interest:

1 They've already expressed some interest, even perhaps by walking into a shop, responding to an email campaign or clicking through from a website.
2 They're totally unaware of your offer and you've stopped them in the street, or cold-called them and captured their attention.

In both situations, the first challenge you face is to hold their attention. Even if they've contacted you with a specific enquiry, they will quickly lose interest if you don't take control and build their interest in short steps. You do this by using open and closed questions.

Here's an example. Imagine that you've had an email enquiry from someone interested in the short cycling breaks your company organizes. You've just had a late cancellation and now have two places on a taster cycling weekend in Yorkshire next month. You're on the phone and, from your opening chat, know they are new to cycling. Here's how the conversation might go:

I've posted you the brochure you ordered online but really wanted to tell you about a last-minute opportunity I thought you might find interesting.

Oh, what's that then?

Well, we have a two-night cycling taster weekend based in Ripon next month and one couple have had to drop out. Would you like to take their place?

Well, as I said, we're new to cycling so might not be able to keep up with an experienced group.

That's no problem; it's a taster weekend, designed for new cyclists. The routes are not too demanding and on quiet lanes through very pretty countryside. How well do you know Yorkshire?

We've been to Yorkshire once or twice actually. But I'm really worried about getting left behind.

How far do you ride your bikes now and how long does it take you?

We tend to ride for around ten miles and that takes just under an hour. Sometimes we ride ten miles out to a nice pub, have lunch and ride back again.

So 20 miles in a day is not impossible for you then?

No, providing it's not a race!

Well, looking at the programme for the taster weekend the longest single ride is 15 miles and we've allowed two hours as there are some great places to take photos along the way. Could you do the weekend 15/16th of next month?

Hmm, let me check my diary.

Can you see how the conversation starts with a statement about a 'last-minute' opportunity? That immediately suggests both urgency, and cost saving. It hooks the customer in and holds their interest while you explore further.

Then a mix of open and closed questions helps you establish just how competent cyclists they are. This is important for you both. It's better not to get the sale than to burden your tour guide with unsuitable people who will spoil the weekend for everyone.

Finally, the customer says that he's going to check the diary. This is the first sign that he's decided that a weekend cycling in Yorkshire is possible. It's called a 'buying signal'. Buying signals show that interest is turning into desire.

IT ALWAYS SEEMS IMPOSSIBLE UNTIL IT'S DONE.

NELSON MANDELA

Creating desire

Imagine that you're on holiday. It's eight in the evening and you're walking along the seafront, past a row of restaurants. You pause to look at the menu outside one of them. A waiter approaches you and invites you inside. But you've already eaten and are just curious, perhaps wondering if this is a place for tomorrow night or later in the week.

No amount of persuasive banter from the waiter will convert your interest into desire. You're no longer hungry. In fact, if she or he persists – and, as we all know, many of them do – you become alienated and, however much you liked the menu, you decide not to return – ever.

Of course, the waiter could have opened by saying, 'Have you eaten yet, sir?', but few actually do. Even though you'd already eaten, you might well have been persuaded to book for another night.

Converting interest into desire is all about making the proposition appear possible, if not likely. I am hungry. I do need to eat. I might as well eat here. I've bought my ticket for the museum and, yes, an extra few pounds for an audio guide might well be helpful. George is the last candidate on what has been a very tiring day of interviews. He's made me smile; he seems to know his stuff. Yes, perhaps he's the man for the job.

When your customer starts saying things like this to themselves, it's time to up the pace and make saying 'yes' as easy as you possibly can. You do this by helping your customer define what saying 'yes' will mean to them. It's probably too easy to close the deal, although it sometimes helps to try. But people don't like to be pushed, so right now is the time to build and quantify that desire.

You can do this by asking qualifying questions that take the customer closer to the big decision. For example: 'Do you prefer our *à la carte* or tourist menu?' 'Did you know that the audio guide to our 'Romans in Britain' exhibition is narrated by so and so?' 'We seem to have a similar sense of humour. Work always seems to go better when people smile; is this a happy workplace?'

The time to switch from stimulating interest to focusing desire is when you begin to notice buying signals. These are selling signposts that point you in the direction you need to go. Buying signals are important so deserve a section of their own, before we move on to the final stage, prompting action.

DO NOT IMPOSE ON OTHERS WHAT YOU YOURSELF DO NOT DESIRE.

CONFUCIUS

Buying signals

Very few people will stop you in mid flow to say that they have decided to buy. But if you are alert and tuned in, you will notice a change in both their language and behaviour once they start to move towards being ready to make a commitment. These signs are called 'buying signals' and are what good salespeople notice and act upon.

As with so many aspects of human behaviour, what is unsaid is far more powerful than what is said. This means that, when you start to notice buying signals, you don't acknowledge them directly. Instead, you become a little more directive and create opportunities for the person to commit. In other words, you start to close the deal. Once someone has decided in their mind to buy, all you have to do is reassure them and ask for the order.

Here are some common buying signals you can look out for:

• handling the product, for example lingering in the driving seat after a car test drive

• asking really detailed questions, for example 'Does it come in blue as well as red?'

• physically leaning forward, smiling, looking more relaxed than during the conversation so far

- looking around for someone to help them
- touching their wallet or purse – a subconscious check that they really can pay today.

Here are some examples you might encounter:

Context: You're in a job interview.

Buying signal: The interviewer says, 'We've just won a contract in Milan and it's giving us a few problems; how good is your Italian.'

What this might mean: If you can sort out the hassle the Italian subcontractors are giving me, the job is yours!

How to respond: 'I worked there as an intern for six months so can do business in Italian, not just enjoy a visit as a tourist.'

Context: You're pitching to your boss for £5,000 to upgrade the dishwasher in your branch of a restaurant chain.

Buying signal: 'So that guy washing up has worked as a barman in the past?'

What this might mean: If this person can serve drinks and won't need replacing in the kitchen, profits will increase.

How to respond: 'Yes, we're lucky to have kept him this long. He's really good with customers and has had the odd hour in the bar, but when we're busy he has to go and run that old dishwasher which means we lose drink sales.'

Context: A furniture showroom

Buying signal: A couple have settled into your three-piece suite and are chatting about what to watch on TV that evening.

What this might mean: They really like the suite and are so comfy they've forgotten they're actually in a shop.

How to respond: 'I can see you like the suite. Have you by any chance brought along the dimensions of your living room?'

Can you see how in each example the salesperson's questioning helps the customer understand a little better how saying 'yes' will be good for them? You speak business – not tourist Italian. You've already tried the guy from the kitchen out in the bar. Have the couple the information you need to show them if the suite will fit in their living room?

> ## ! Understand selling
>
> If you pay good attention to them, people will usually unwittingly let you know when they are ready to start talking seriously about making a decision.

'THE ART OF LEADERSHIP IS SAYING NO, NOT SAYING YES. IT IS VERY EASY TO SAY YES.'

TONY BLAIR

Prompting action

One of the biggest differences between a sales and a social conversation is that, when selling, there is a clearly defined goal. You want to gain commitment and do this in a timely way, rather than spend ages talking to someone who is not going to agree to anything. Asking for commitment is a good way of bringing a sales conversation closer to a positive conclusion.

If you ask for the order, one of two things happens. The customer says 'yes' or 'no'. Actually, they usually say 'yes if' or 'no because'. Both are positive because they show you exactly what's stopping them from making the commitment you want. Very people just say 'yes', unless the purchase is very modest or the decision very easy to make.

Once you've been though the previous steps of the sales conversation, you have a pretty good idea what the customer values most about what you are proposing. Now the time has come to close the deal.

Closing is the part of the sales process that people fear the most. The reason for this is simple. By asking for a firm commitment, you run the risk of your proposition being rejected. Worse, there's the irrational fear that you've misread all the positive buying signals. You're afraid that asking for the order will provoke an outburst directed at you personally.

Of course, this negative reaction rarely, if ever, happens. People do not like to cause offence and so will try very hard to tactfully turn you down when you try to close. If someone is going to be angry, they'll have been getting angry for a while. And as nobody makes a good decision when annoyed, angry people are best left alone. You can always reschedule the meeting.

Closing

You close a deal by asking a closed question. That you may remember is one that demands a 'yes' or 'no' answer. As you've just read, what usually happens is that you usually get 'yes if' or 'no because'. Both answers enable you to deal with the objection (that's what they're called) and, having resolved it, close again. In fact, there's an old selling adage that refers to the ABC of selling – always be closing! The skill is to do this with subtlety and good humour.

If you Google 'closing techniques', you'll see that every sales guru or business advice website has some favourite techniques. My advice is not to worry about the variations on the closing theme. Instead, simply do what feels right and works for you each time.

Closing is covered in a lot more detail further into the book, particularly in Chapters 9, 14 and 18. For now, here are some ways that you can gain commitment from others:

- **Create urgency or scarcity** – there's nothing like a deadline to focus the buyer on making up his or her mind: 'This is the last one at the old price', 'We've been able to get this one, but there's a long order book and it'll be months before the next batch appear.'

- **Provide alternatives of which one is more specific than the other** – 'Would you like the green one, or one of the other colours?', 'Can you see me tomorrow afternoon or sometime next week?'

- **Assume that you have the order** – 'So we've been talking about three nights' dinner, bed and breakfast from 1 June in a garden-facing room. Can I have the 16-digit number on your card, please?'

The last of these requires a little more confidence but, for the dithering decision maker, usually generates a huge sigh of relief.

'EVERYONE LIVES BY SELLING SOMETHING.'

ROBERT LOUIS STEVENSON

Dealing with objections

Objections are the reasons people give for not giving you the commitment you are asking for. Usually people say no because:

- they are not yet fully convinced
- they want more time to think
- they are not the decision maker and need to get the decision approved
- they really do mean 'no'.

When someone says 'no', the first thing you must do is ask why. A simple open question such as 'Why do you say that?' may be all that is needed to identify the barrier. Once you know what's holding them back, you can deal with the objection and ask for commitment once more.

Professional salespeople ask for the order long before they know the customer is ready to agree. This is called 'trial closing' and enables the salesperson to focus on the features and benefits of most interest. It makes a sales conversation more concise but, done badly, can appear forceful.

Remember that, once you've identified the objection, you need to use open and closed questions to understand, then solve, the concern. Here's an example to show you what I mean:

So you've heard how investing £500 in a new coffee machine for the office will save time and energy. Can I place the order please?

No.

Ah, so what makes you say that?

Well, I had set aside the money to redecorate the meeting room, which I think looks a little tired.

Tell me, why do you think the meeting room is so important?

It's where we take prospective customer, and, if it's scruffy, they'll be put off buying.

So what's really important to you is to make sure our visitors are happy?

Yes.

Which do you think they would prefer, a nice room and instant coffee or a slightly tired room with freshly ground coffee? Oh and perhaps flowers from the supermarket on the table.

OK, I see what you mean. Will you take responsibility for the coffee machine and making sure that we have flowers when visitors are expected?

Sure, so I'll order the coffee machine then.

Yes, OK.

Can you see how open and closed questions enabled the person selling to identify the objection and explain how it could be overcome? Asking whether the coffee or the decor was more important might be considered risky but, had the decor been chosen, more questioning would have found out why.

❗ Understand selling

Never take no for an answer until you have fully explored and perhaps challenged the reasons behind the refusal.

'FOR A WHILE, I WAS SAYING "NO" WAY TOO OFTEN. I TURNED DOWN *AN OFFICER AND A GENTLEMAN*, *SPLASH* AND *MIDNIGHT EXPRESS*.'

JOHN TRAVOLTA

In this chapter you've discovered:

- that selling is a four-stage process: attention, interest, desire and action (AIDA)
- that listening carefully and watching body language will give you clues about what the other person is thinking but not necessarily saying
- that it's good to check if someone's in the market for what you are selling early on
- that, when someone says 'no', they often just mean they're not yet convinced.

5.

Succeeding – how to exceed expectations

Goal setting

Most people in sales jobs have targets to achieve. The car dealership has an agreed volume of new cars to sell each month. The baker wants to sell all of the bread he baked that morning. The manager of the squash club knows how many members she needs to cover running costs.

If you simply want to be more successful at work, you will need to sell yourself and your ideas, but without clearly defined sales targets to achieve. This is why it is important to have goals for your life and career, as well as for any products or services you are responsible for selling.

Whatever you are selling, you will sell with more conviction, energy and enthusiasm if you have a clear image of what getting that sale will mean to you. Moreover, it will help you enormously to have a clear vision for your long-term future.

Once you have long-term goals, you can develop a strategy to achieve them. Then you can use a range of tactics to make sure that you follow the strategy and realize your vision. For example:

Jane works as a florist. Her employer has a good rapport with a number of local hotels and funeral directors. They provide much of the work Jane does. Funeral flowers is an area that really interests Jane and she has a long-term goal to start her own business specializing in this area. She wants the opportunity to develop her creativity further than her current job allows. She also wants to be her own boss.

Jane's vision, then, is to become a self-employed florist specializing in funeral flowers.

Her strategy might be to build her own network of funeral directors, perhaps introducing them initially as new customers to her employer's firm. Her tactics and timeline might be:

• **Year one** – Join and become an active member of business networks attended by funeral directors. By selling herself and building her profile, she will develop her own network of business contacts. She contacts a local enterprise agency and does a start-up course to learn what's involved. She writes a business plan.

- **Year two** – Organize a funeral floristry competition to associate her name with innovative funeral flower arrangement. She sells a sponsorship package to the funeral director she thinks has the greatest potential of being her first big customer. She makes sure that the competition is a success.

- **Year three** – Her youngest child has changed schools and she's ready to start her business. The funeral director that sponsored the competition agrees to back her and she starts to look for premises. By coincidence, her boss's husband takes early retirement from a senior police job. She asks her boss whether she'd like to retire, too. With backing from the supportive funeral director, she buys the business.

> SERENDIPITY ALWAYS REWARDS THE PREPARED.
>
> KATORI HALL (CONTEMPORARY AMERICAN PLAYWRIGHT)

If setting personal goals is new to you, here are four pointers to help you:

1 Work out what you want your future to look like; don't just accept what you think others expect of you.

2 Set bold, audacious goals, then show how step by step you can achieve them.

3 Write down your goals and the steps to achieving them in the present, not future tense ('It's 2020 and I am…' etc.).

4 Accept that every setback will strengthen your resolve and contribute to your success.

! Think goals

Selling will be far easier if you know what success means to you.

Planning

Having set goals, you next need to plan to achieve them. This sounds obvious, but without a plan too much is left to chance. Writing a career or business plan will help you identify what needs to happen when in order for you to reach your ultimate goal. The shorter the steps you define, the clearer it will become to see exactly what needs to be done.

But let's focus on pure sales planning and how to make sure that you achieve your sales target. You may be surprised to learn that hitting sales targets is as much about monitoring some simple arithmetic rations as it is about your ability to close deals.

Let me use a simple example to explain:

- Imagine that you work for an estate agent. Your job is to sell houses. Taking an average house price of £250,000 and a 1 per cent commission rate, it's easy to work out that each sale makes your firm £2,500.
- Your monthly sales target is to generate £10,000 of income for the firm. This means selling on average four houses.
  - Now we need to look at some ratios. Let's suppose that on average:
  - each house you put on the market attracts 50 enquiries
  - 20 per cent of enquiries generate a viewing (10 viewings)
  - 10 per cent of viewings result in a sale (1 sale).
  - Now you need to sell four houses a month. That means you need to generate:
  - 40 viewings, because 10 per cent of them result is a sale
  - 200 enquiries, because 20 per cent of them lead to a viewing.
- What this means is that the most important thing to achieve is enquiries. That's because (to use the example), if you only generate 150 in a month, you're almost certain to sell only three houses.

This technique is called 'backward planning' and is used extensively in call centres to monitor sales performance. What backward planning helps you do is monitor performance over time. You can do more of what works well and less of what doesn't deliver the results you need. Selling is not just about the face-to-face meeting. It's about the whole process of marketing and selling.

We'll cover the marketing aspects of selling in later chapters. It's important because, clearly, the more effectively you promote yourself, your ideas or your products and services, the better the quality of the enquiries you will generate. This, in turn, means you will sell to more of the people you present, too. That means less time is wasted trying to sell to people who are not going to buy.

> 'PLANS ARE NOTHING; PLANNING IS EVERYTHING.'
>
> DWIGHT D. EISENHOWER

! Think goals

The more effectively you generate good-quality enquiries, the less time you will need to spend face-to-face selling.

Making it real

For about a year, I sold financial services products on a commission-only basis. It was at a time when that industry was not as tightly regulated as it is today. It was perhaps the most sales-intensive role I have ever had. Everyone I met had the potential to become a client. It was very target-driven; there was quite literally a league table of commission income listed on a whiteboard next to the coffee machine. It was updated every afternoon. The environment was fiercely competitive.

Looking back, I realize that it was a great opportunity to refresh my selling skills. It was also a fascinating opportunity to see how, in a highly target-driven sales setting, both salespeople and managers 'made it real'.

You see, backward planning was at the very heart of the sales process in that office. We measured and compared our performance ratios. Great emphasis was placed on generating enquiries and leads, either by referrals or cold-calling. One evening a week we would all be in the office together making cold calls to people at home. You can imagine how tough that was.

What made it real was that we were all encouraged to have a very clear idea how we would spend the commission those leads would generate. Many would have a photo of their dream car – or, more likely, of their children – on the desk in front of them when they were generating their next week's appointments.

It took a lot of cold calls to make an appointment to visit someone, but once in their living room you'd find that perhaps one in three would become a client. That meant we could calculate how many appointments we needed to make each week.

If we said that each new client was worth £900 in commission and you had to visit three people to generate one client, then, in reality, each visit had a value of £900/3, or £300. But, to generate each appointment, you'd perhaps have to cold-call 50 people. So each cold call would be worth £6. If you wanted to earn £1,800 in the next week, you knew you had to make 150 cold calls. It was that simple.

I'm pretty sure that you will never find yourself in such a harsh selling job. But the lessons I learned there have, in a more palatable form, influenced my selling structure and planning ever since. Once you have translated your sales goals and conversion ratios into a backward plan, you can put a value on every step of the lead generation and conversion process.

The best salespeople always make it real, always know the value to them of each activity and always have a bold vision for what they want for themselves and their families.

! **Think goals**

Remember the old sales adage that 'Every no brings you closer to a yes!'

Rewarding success

It has to be said that some sales forces still employ carrot-and-stick tactics to motivate their salespeople. Sales rewards and incentives used to be very common. I once attended the FA Cup Final because I had sold more fertilizer than my colleagues. The problem with this is, of course, that it encourages rivalry and, at times, intense competition between people who should be pulling together as one team.

But, that said, rewarding your success when your sales efforts bear fruit is important. Here are some simple things you can do to give you the push to give selling the priority it deserves in your life:

- Reward yourself for making follow-up phone calls with a treat after so many – perhaps a chocolate biscuit and cup of coffee after ten calls.
- Take your partner out to dinner after you've given your best at a promotion interview, even if you did not get the job. You'll inevitably have learned from the experience.
- If you employ people who can contribute directly to your sales success, consider paying them commission.
- Finally, don't forget to reward those who introduce you to new customers, or open the door for you to meet someone able to influence your career success. Even saying thank you and saying how you got on with the introduction is better than giving no feedback at all.

'CALL IT WHAT YOU WILL, INCENTIVES ARE WHAT GET PEOPLE TO WORK HARDER.'

NIKITA KHRUSHCHEV

Keeping in touch

As I've just hinted, people introduced to you by existing customers can be a lucrative source of new business. There are two reasons for this. First, they will be endorsing and recommending you, which counts for a lot. Second, their enthusiasm for their recent purchase or decision will be infectious. If you buy a new car, you're usually keen to show it off to friends. If the dealership has impressed you, you're likely to recommend them. If the salesperson offers you an incentive to bring your friends for a test drive, you might just do it – but only if you have friends thinking of buying a new car.

You will be more successful if you:

- always ask for referrals and make it easy for people who buy from you to recommend you to others
- build and keep in touch with a wide network of people
- maintain a high public/online profile so that people who hear about you can find you easily.

Techniques for keeping in touch are covered in more detail in Chapters 9 (Networking) and 16 (Prospecting).

> **!** **Think goals**
>
> Success is not only about whom you know but who knows you, too.

In this chapter you've discovered:

- that motivating yourself to sell will be easier if you have clear personal goals
- that it is important to plan backwards from the goal to the activity needed to achieve it
- that selling is all about people, particularly people recommending you to others.

PART II

Selling yourself

6.

Planning – work out what you want to achieve and why

Let's talk about you

The most important thing you will ever sell is yourself. People will want to spend time with you, work with you, hire you, support you and buy from you if they like, respect and value you. This section of the book, therefore, is focused on you.

We all find it difficult to sell ourselves. This is partly because most of us are modest and find self-promotion uncomfortable. It is often also because we're not quite sure what we are selling. Self-help experts will say that many of us go through life without much direction.

We are born, go to school, get a job, have relationships, develop hobbies, get old, retire and then die. As we reach each turning point, we choose what appears to be the best route ahead, basing our decision on what we can see in front of us. Few look beyond the immediate and obvious. Most are content with their lives, but perhaps never quite realize their full potential.

Of course, it all depends where we are starting from. Those born into wealthy families who attend expensive private schools and good universities still find it easier to become government ministers or senior business leaders than those who don't.

The twentieth-century psychologist Abraham Maslow developed a theory he called the 'hierarchy of needs'. It listed in order of importance the things we all need. His point was that, unless we had the basics, we would not be interested in anything more. Here's his list:

1 **Food, water and shelter** – this is all that matters if you're cold and hungry.
2 **Personal safety** – if you feel threatened, little else matters to you.
3 **Love** – once we feel safe and comfortable, we need to be with others.

4 **Esteem** – we all want people to like and respect us.

5 **Self-actualization** – only when we have 1–4 covered can we have and realize our dreams.

If you compare the homeless person on the street with the wealthy philanthropist who funds a night shelter, you will see how Maslow's hierarchy works. The homeless person can't really plan beyond tonight. The philanthropist has material and emotional wealth, which gives him the freedom to consider others and help meet his needs. Interestingly, many philanthropists have direct personal experience of the social issue they set out to resolve.

Before you can sell yourself effectively, you have to know what success looks like to you. Where you are starting from clearly matters, but not as much as it does to have a clear idea of where you want to go.

> 'IF WE DID ALL THE THINGS WE WERE CAPABLE OF DOING, WE WOULD LITERALLY ASTOUND OURSELVES.'
>
> THOMAS EDISON

! Planning to succeed

We are all unique and so have different ambitions and expectations from life. None is better than yours, although many will be different.

Passion

There is nothing quite as persuasive as a passionate presentation. The more passionate you are, the more enthusiastic you will be and the more others will feel compelled to support you. Passion is the fire that fuels success. It drives you to achieve, even in the face of opposition and adversity.

Remember that the decision to buy anything is emotionally driven, then self-justified by logic. If you are passionate about what you want to do, others will be far more likely to help you – providing, of course, that there is some benefit for them in helping you, even if it's just seeing you succeed.

You can't just wake up one morning and decide to be passionate about your job. You need an emotional connection and a very real belief that what you are doing is going to make the world a better place. People can be passionate about almost anything. Personal passion is often derived from your past. For example:

- **Louis Pasteur** was driven to research how diseases were transmitted after losing three of his children to typhoid.
- **Alexander Graham Bell** had a profoundly deaf wife and invented the telephone because he wanted to make it easier for her to communicate.
- **James Dyson** made more than 5,000 prototypes for his bag-less vacuum cleaner before perfecting the design. He was passionate about challenging what he saw as inefficient technology.

If you are going to be successful, you need to find your passion and pursue it. People follow passionate people.

- If you are passionate about golf, others will be more likely to pay a round with you than if you only joined the club to meet the 'right' people.
- If you passionately want to be a school head teacher (and not just for the money), you will find it easier to succeed in getting the jobs you need to build the career experience you need.
- If ever since you were a small child you've wanted to be a farmer, you'll find a way to achieve it, even if not in the way you first imagined.

'IF YOU WANT TO DO SOMETHING DIFFERENT, YOU'RE GOING TO COME UP AGAINST A LOT OF NAYSAYERS.'

JAMES DYSON

Success

To achieve success, you first have to define it. In selling terms, this is about understanding your features and how they will benefit others as well as yourself. Remember that we can achieve very little on our own. We all rely on winning the support of others to achieve personal success.

Because we humans are so versatile, we have to make choices about the direction we want to go. For example, with training, most people could become a bus driver, a chef or a minister of religion. But if you hated driving, you'd not enjoy driving buses. If you liked being outdoors, you'd hate spending your life in a kitchen. And, if you had no faith, being a minister of any kind would be very uncomfortable.

Here are some ways you might define personal success:

• passing your driving test
• the amount of money you earn and are able to save
• a good relationship with someone who's just right for you
• work you enjoy with an organization that is secure and expanding
• winning an athletics competition
• seeing your children do better than you
• being able to retire at 65.

Can you see how, in each example, your success depends on others helping you. None of the above will be sure to happen if you leave it to chance.

• To pass your driving test, you need money for lessons and a good instructor.
• To be well paid, you need a job, a boss or, if self-employed, customers.
• A good relationship needs there to be someone who feels for you as strongly as you feel for them.
• For work to be enjoyable, you need to be doing something you find interesting, not just financially rewarding.
• To win a race, you might need a coach, or team members who encourage you to push yourself hard.
• For your children to excel, you need them to have good teachers.
• To retire at 65, you need enough income to be able to save over a long period of time.

What's more, to enlist the support of others, you will probably need to help them see the benefit to them in helping you achieve success. For example, if you are 18 and want driving lessons, the benefit to your parents for funding this might be freedom from going out late at night to give you a lift home from late-night gigs after the buses have stopped running. Selling the idea of paying for your driving lessons might involve helping them see and even quantify the benefits of going to bed early on a Saturday night!

'CHASE YOUR PASSION, NOT YOUR PENSION.'

DENIS WAITLEY (AMERICAN AUTHOR AND MOTIVATIONAL SPEAKER)

Working SMART

People will be more likely to support you, in other words to buy into you and your plans, if they appear achievable. Of course, your selling skills will help, but you do need to be realistic. For example, I recently met some unemployed 16-year-olds at a project supporting youngsters excluded from school. One told me he wanted to be paid a lot of money to test video games, and another that he hoped one day to own his own restaurant, but right now had signed up to become an apprentice chef.

Which do you think I felt I could help? The first lad had a vision of thoughts, but no idea how to go about making it real. He just wanted money and to be able to play video games all day. The second had both a vision and, more importantly, had recognized the need to take it one step at a time. Furthermore, he asked me whether I could help with something very specific, finding a restaurant which would hire him as an apprentice. I was able to use my contacts to secure him an interview.

What the second student had done was to set himself some SMART objectives. Smart is an acronym standing for:

- **S**pecific – the more specific the goal, the easier it is to describe and achieve
- **M**easurable – because then you can quantify the benefits of achievement
- **A**ttainable – perhaps step by step rather than all in one giant leap
- **R**ealistic – no one will help you tackle what to them appears impossible
- **T**imely – without a timescale, things will slip.

The budding restaurateur didn't realize he was being SMART, but he was!

- **S**pecific – to realize his long-term goal, he needs a restaurant to hire him.
- **M**easurable – it will be easy to see when he's got a job.
- **A**ttainable – there are lots of restaurants looking for staff.
- **R**ealistic – he has enough qualifications to start an apprenticeship.
- **T**imely – his course would start in September so he has a deadline.

Take time to reflect on the things you want to achieve at home, work or in business. How easy is it right now to describe them in SMART terms? Remember that the 'smarter' your goals, the easier it will be to sell them to those whose help you need to achieve them.

'YOUR MIND KNOWS ONLY SOME THINGS. YOUR INNER VOICE, YOUR INSTINCT, KNOWS EVERYTHING. IF YOU LISTEN TO WHAT YOU KNOW INSTINCTIVELY, IT WILL ALWAYS LEAD YOU DOWN THE RIGHT PATH.'

HENRY WINKLER

! Planning to succeed

The greater your passion, the clearer you define success and the smarter the steps you plan, the easier it will be for others to see why they should help you.

Doing your thing

To be really persuasive and take others where you want them to go, you have to be confident you are on the right track yourself. Once you have found your passion and defined what success looks like for you, you will, without realizing it, become more effective at selling yourself and your ideas to others. You will find yourself becoming more:

- **active** – taking on more challenges and encouraging others to join you in your quests
- **excited** – because what you are doing is motivating you and, by osmosis, those around you, too

- **focused** – with the determination that comes from having clear goals in mind
- **enthusiastic** – driven to share your passion and enable others to become enthusiastic, too
- **courageous** – willing to take risks and inspire others to do the same
- **happy** – because you're doing what you feel is important – happiness is infectious!

Your game plan

Now, having thought about where you are in your life, what you feel most passionate about and how you define personal success, you might feel ready to prepare your game plan. Take some time out and use these questions to help you define what it is you really want to achieve:

- In five years' time, what do you want your life to look like?
- To create that future, what are the most important three things you need to achieve this year?
- For each of those three things, who are the people you need to persuade to help you achieve them?
- What are the measurable benefits for them in helping you succeed?
- What is a realistic timescale within which you can have sought their support?
- How will you celebrate when you have won their support to achieve those three key short-term goals?

! **Planning to succeed**

Writing down your goals and pinning the list where you can easily see them will give you the periodic pushes you need to actually do something about achieving them.

In this chapter you've discovered:

- that ambition emerges only once life's basic needs are covered
- that the stronger your passion, the more powerfully you will persuade.

7.
Communicating – getting your message across

Effective communication

Humans have always lived in communities. In ancient times, survival depended upon being able to communicate effectively. We had to warn one another of approaching danger and hunt collectively for food. We lived in nomadic interdependent tribes and, as a consequence, tended not to have complex conversations. The pace of life was too hectic for that.

Instead, we relied upon body language and shouted warnings or encouragement to know what was going on around us. Much of the time it was the tone of voice, rather than the words used, that conveyed the message. In fact, language itself evolved quite late in our journey.

It's been said by scientists studying human behaviour that:

- 55 per cent of our communication is non-verbal
- 35 per cent is conveyed by tone of voice
- 10 per cent is by the words we use.

So you can see that the words you use are actually the least important, at least when speaking. It's why we quickly sense when someone is telling us a lie. It's also why we can tell when someone is not convinced themselves that what they are suggesting to us is the best option for us.

A writer, on the other hand, has to convey tone of voice and feeling using just words on paper or a screen. (We'll end this chapter with some notes on writing effectively.)

Let's work through each of the kinds of communication in turn.

'THREE THINGS CANNOT BE LONG HIDDEN: THE SUN, THE MOON, AND THE TRUTH.'

BUDDHA

Body language

We've already covered a little about body language in Chapter 1, so let's now go a little deeper. It really is important to become aware of, and able to influence, your body language. If how you appear and what people see do not match, you will appear to lack confidence or, worse, seem to be insincere.

The good news is that, if you are passionate about the subject, it will be reflected in your body language. You will automatically appear positive and in tune with your message. Enthusiasm encourages you to stand straight, show interest and appear convincing.

If you're not sure about the importance of body language, think back to the last time you queued to buy something, perhaps a ticket at a railway station. When you reach the window, it's often clear that the person on the other side is not at all interested in you.

Instead, they're focused on dealing with the queue. They will probably be slouched in their chair, not hold eye contact and speak in a monotone. They may not even look you in the eye when they hand you your ticket and return your credit card. By then, their interest has already switched to the person standing waiting impatiently behind you.

Of course, not everyone who sells tickets behaves in this way. But my bet is that you will have experienced indifference of this kind and remember how it makes you feel. When you're selling anything, you need above all to be enthusiastic.

In Chapter 1 you saw this table:

Positive body language	Negative body language
Smiling	Scowling
Standing tall	Slouching
Making eye contact	Avoiding eye contact
Speaking slowly and clearly	Speaking quickly
Open, gesturing arms	Folded arms

By being aware of, and emphasizing, positive body language you will automatically appear more confident and self-assured. This can be difficult if you are nervous about the meeting you are about to have. Perhaps it's an interview for a job you desperately want, in which case you might be more than a little nervous.

Here are some ways you can avoid looking nervous:

• Arrive half an hour early and take a walk. This will make sure you're there on time and the walk will help you calm down. The exercise will help you stand tall and breathe easily.

• Smile when you enter the room or are greeted at the door. Notice how, when you smile first, others usually smile back. Smiles take tension out of meetings.

• Make an effort to keep good eye contact and, if you can, hold it when asked a question until you have answered it. It will make you appear more confident.

• Take a moment and a breath or two before answering a question. It's OK to pause for thought.

• Keep your hands in view and let them help you make your point. Hand gestures are an important part of body language and something we all do naturally, until we start thinking about it.

Body language is a two-way conversation. As your awareness grows, you will increasingly read the body language of those around you. It is polite to acknowledge and return the gesture. This is called 'mirroring'.

Mirroring is how we instinctively show that we are in tune with the person we're talking with. I smile at you and you smile back. If you don't, I might ask you what's up. In fact, if I don't and simply plough on with what I want to say, I risk alienating you. Body language is all about wavelength, and mirroring is how we confirm we are on the same wavelength.

Imagine that you are in a job interview. There are three on the panel and the interview is drawing to a close. You look at the panel and see that one is nodding in agreement with what you are saying. You nod back in acknowledgement then look to the other two. You know that you've won over one of the panel members. It's time to focus harder on the other two.

While reading and responding to body language in a small group are important, in a large group it can be very misleading. That's because, unless you're connecting strongly with someone, you simply don't know what else is influencing their posture and responses. For example:

You might think	They might actually
Someone looking at their lap has lost interest in what you have to say	Be tweeting what you said because they want to share it before they forget
Two people in the room looking angry means you've offended them	Have just had an argument and be sulking
Someone leaps up excitedly and cheers and you think you've persuaded them	Have just had a text to say they've become a grandmother!

The most important thing to remember about body language is to be aware of it but not to worry too much about it. Rather like riding a bike, this is easy to do once you know how, but difficult if you try to predict and manage every move.

'WEAR A SMILE AND HAVE FRIENDS; WEAR A SCOWL AND HAVE WRINKLES.'

GEORGE ELIOT

! **Communicate well**

Always respond to what body language tells you. It can be more honest than what someone is saying to you.

How you speak

It is said that your tone of speech is three times more influential than the words you are saying. If you saw someone weeping and they said, 'I'm so happy today,' you'd not believe them. Equally, if someone was putting on a jolly voice when actually deeply unhappy, you'd spot that, too.

How we speak when we're selling has a big influence on how successful we will be. It's not about our accent or voice, but how we use our voice. When you think about it, we can tell a lot about what someone else is thinking from the way they speak to us.

For example:

- Speaking in a flat monotone suggests you are bored and not at all interested.
- Your voice will rise to a higher pitch when challenging something you don't believe.
- Speaking too quickly implies urgency and also perhaps that you are not confident.
- Switching from comfortable conversation to more formal presentation means it's time for business.
- Stressing key points as you say them gives them added punch and helps people remember them.
- Answering questions abruptly and snappily says you are angry.

All of the above are obvious when you think about them. The point is that most of us don't think about them, until, that is, we read a book about selling! It's not just about influencing the way you speak. It's perhaps more important to understand how others are feeling and respond to the underlying cause. The better you become at reading people, the greater your success.

You can influence your tone of voice by:

- being aware of how you are speaking and how this might be interpreted
- using language you feel comfortable with, rather than 'business speak'
- standing up and moving around
- being physically fit, rather than short of breath
- emphasizing the words and phrases that matter most.

A good way to hear how tone of voice can convey meaning is to listen to dialogue on the radio. Interviews in particular will provide good opportunities to compare what is being said with how it is being said. Radio plays can illustrate well how professional actors can use tone of voice to convey emotion.

'WE OFTEN REFUSE TO ACCEPT AN IDEA MERELY BECAUSE THE TONE OF VOICE IN WHICH IT HAS BEEN EXPRESSED IS UNSYMPATHETIC TO US.'

FRIEDRICH NIETZSCHE

What you say

Much of this book focuses on what you say. That's because selling is all about using words to influence decision making. When you sell, it's important that you speak confidently, clearly and, above all else, positively.

The challenge we all face is that it's always easier to see the negative before the positive. Our attention is always drawn to the things we consider wrong with our lives. We take for granted and ignore what is going well for us. To sell successfully, however, we need to work on developing a more positive outlook.

The simple fact is that people prefer to be with, to employ and to do business with people who are positive. So, even if you have doubts, and we all do, it's good to introduce more positive words into your vocabulary.

A good way to set the scene for a positive conversation is to make your opening positive. Often, if you meet a friend in the street and ask, 'How are you today?', many will say 'Not too bad' instead of 'Really good, thank you.' Having a positive response to the question 'How are you?' and using it often will make sure that your meetings start positively.

You will also appear more positive if you use assertive, positive words rather than those that hit at doubt or uncertainty. For example:

Uncertain	Certain
I wonder if you'd enjoy this one, madam?	I just know you'll love this one, madam!
Would you be interested in a shave as well as a haircut today?	A shave as well as a haircut will set you up perfectly for the evening. Which shall I do first?
I think I could do that.	I know I can do that.

Clearly, you should not overstate what's possible. However, making a positive effort to avoid words that hint at doubt will make you appear more confident and positive.

Words to avoid	Words to use
Wonder	Know
Hope	Expect
Possibly	Certainly
Maybe	Definitely
Hopefully	Surely

When structuring sentences, it helps to emphasize the positive and minimize the negative. For example:

- 'So you're confident I can do everything the job requires, apart from the fact I have yet to pass my driving test?'
- 'You liked the flat, especially the view, the kitchen and the bathroom, but are worried whether there'll be enough storage space?'

Gaining agreement that these (minor) points are the only problems, you have only to solve them to get the deal. So, having a date for your driving test, or knowing where you can get some nice cupboards for the flat, might make all the difference between a 'yes' and a 'no'.

Finally, the most important point of all: the more you use the words 'you' and 'your', the more successful you will be. We all like to talk about ourselves but, when we're selling, it's the other person who becomes more important.

Advertising copywriters use the word 'you' as much as they can and good salespeople do the same. For example:

Me phrases (to avoid)	You phrases (to include)
I love baking these cakes.	You'll love eating these cakes.
I've put 30 years of my life into making this perfect.	You'll be reassured to know it took a lifetime to make this perfect.
I really want this job.	You won't be disappointed if you give me the job.

POSITIVE THINKING WILL LET YOU DO EVERYTHING BETTER THAN NEGATIVE THINKING WILL.

ZIG ZIGLAR

Know, think and do

If you are going to sell anything, particularly yourself, you need to communicate effectively. That means much more than just speaking clearly. It also means thinking before you speak rather than simply saying the first thing that comes into your head. Most importantly, it means thinking about what you want the other person to know, think and do as a result of meeting you.

In fact, it's useful as you prepare for any kind of communication, written as well as verbal, to plan in advance what you want the other person to:

• **know** – the information you want them to gain from you
• **think** – the opinion this encourages them to form
• **do** – the action that you hope will result.

Imagine, for example, that I am trying to persuade you to come for a run with me. If all I do is talk enthusiastically about my passion for running and share my personal best running times, you might well decide that I am too competitive and will leave you behind. To avoid embarrassment, you will probably decline the offer. That's because you:

• **know** – I'm a keen and competitive runner
• **think** – I'll be faster than you and will make you feel silly when I pull ahead
• **do** – say 'no' because you don't see any benefit in bolstering my ego by losing.

But my goal is not to show off but to persuade you to run with me. To do this, I need to think about what I can say that will encourage you to come for that jog. So using the 'know, think, do' structure, I might tell you that I love running and enjoy it far more with a running buddy than on my own. I might also say that I don't mind how far we run, or at what pace. Lastly, I might say that I know a great café we could visit afterwards for coffee and cake.

So now you:

- **know** – that I enjoy the conversation as well as the run and won't leave you behind
- **think** – that you'll set the pace and so not be left behind
- **do** – say 'yes' because a gentle run followed by coffee and cake actually sounds rather nice.

By being clear about my objective, to persuade you to run with me, I succeed only when I focus on what's in it for you rather than what's in it for me.

! **Communicate well**

It's surprisingly easy to talk people out of something. Focus on helping them to know why and to think that saying 'yes' to your proposition is their best option.

What you write

Many of the rules and guidelines about effective speech apply equally to written communication. You need to use upbeat, positive language rather than write negatively. It's also even more important to avoid using jargon, acronyms or overlong words.

In fact, you have to work extra hard to make your writing positive. That's because, for most people, the default is to see the downside and write negatively, sometimes without even noticing. When you are writing, your anxieties and concerns can easily slip into your writing. Your reader will quickly pick them up unless you spot them first and edit them out.

Effective sales writing is always:

- **positive** – focusing on the possible rather than the problems
- **assertive** – confident, informed and constructive
- **assumptive** – assuming the reader is going to agree
- **empathic** – written with the reader, rather than the writer, in mind.

As important as the words you use is the way you punctuate your writing. Punctuation gives your reader the opportunity to pause for breath when reading aloud. More importantly, perhaps, is that it gives your reader time to pause for thought. For example, when writing this book I have:

- kept sentence length short, with few longer than 15 words
- kept each point separate and distinct within its own paragraph
- used bullet point lists to make it easy for you to find the most important content.

In addition to these, don't forget to use pictures, graphs and even video to illustrate your writing. There's nothing to say that you shouldn't create a YouTube video in which you say why you're the person for the job, then add a hyperlink to it in your CV. Selling is not about following rules but achieving results!

When writing emails, you can break conventions – using dashes rather than commas to break up text. You can also use hyperlinks to pages that support your point, so that your message can be short, succinct and very clear in what it is asking the reader to do.

! Communicate well

As a rule of thumb, if you have to look up what a word means, it's the wrong word. Keep your writing simple, focused and explicit.

In this chapter you've discovered:

- that non-verbal communication is more influential than what you say
- that thinking and talking more positively are something most of us can benefit from
- that following the 'know, think and do' principle is vital if you want to persuade others to do what you want them to do.

8.
Profile – how to present yourself, on paper and online

Understanding your brand

Selling yourself becomes a lot easier if people have heard of you and know something of what you stand for. In other words, people will be more inclined to say 'yes' to you if they have a clear understanding of what you are all about. The best way to think about this is to consider your personal brand.

The UK Government's Intellectual Property Office describes a brand as 'a trade name, a sign, symbol, slogan or anything that is used to identify and distinguish a specific product, service or business'. But, if you think about it, exactly the same description might be applied to you. For example:

Business brands have	Personal brands have	Examples
Trade names	Nicknames	Footballer Paul Gascoigne = Gazza Margaret Thatcher = the Iron Lady
Signs/symbols	Style/appearance	Designer Karl Lagerfeld wears very high collars Marilyn Monroe had a very specific 'look'
Slogans	Catch phrases	Sir Alan Sugar, business magnate from *The Apprentice* (UK), 'You're fired!' Sir Bruce Forsyth, TV presenter and entertainer, 'Didn't he/she do well!'

People who are well known and enjoy a high public profile usually work at developing and maintaining their brand. It not only helps them become more memorable but also helps them influence what they are remembered for. And, if you have a name that's difficult to spell, such as Gascoigne, it makes you easier to find, too!

The Government IP Office goes further in their description of brand. They say that a brand can also be 'promise of an experience'. It is this promise that your personal brand needs to encapsulate. What experience can others expect when they meet or consult you? How does your expertise and experience translate into value for others?

Your personal brand needs to:

• focus on your key strengths
• be memorable and perhaps even visual
• capture how you want others to see you
• explain why you are the 'go to' person for anyone interested in your subject.

Remember that sometimes less can actually deliver you more. Indian politician Mahatma Gandhi made a big deal about wearing very simple clothes. He also used a spinning wheel, illustrating his connection with the simple life lived by most of his people. Similarly, and more recently, Pope Francis shunned the palatial Vatican apartment used by his predecessor in favour of something far more basic. Both Gandhi and the Pope did this to illustrate that, while they were world leaders, they had not lost sight of how most people lived their lives.

To illustrate this and make it easier for you to define your own brand, here's the story of my own brand: 'the barefoot entrepreneur'.

My challenge was that, as a successful social entrepreneur, innovator and business author, everyone had heard of me but few fully understood how I could help them. I hired a summer postgraduate intern to explore my marketplace and my position within it and suggest how I could become easier to find.

His research identified the five features and benefits people most value in my work:

1 **independent** – impartial and not swayed by the agendas of those around me
2 **challenging** – willing to look beyond the obvious
3 **entrepreneurial** – able to make things happen, not just suggest them
4 **networked** – with links to people able to influence project success
5 **sensitive** – empathic, passionate, connects emotionally with projects.

Two of these stood out: the entrepreneurial energy and sensitivity to the needs and feelings of others. This led to the phrase 'barefoot entrepreneur' – 'barefoot' because the word implies sensitivity, vulnerability and humility, balancing the more forceful entrepreneurial skills.

The branding is supported by photographs of me barefoot. Indeed, I often speak barefoot at conferences, emerging on to the stage in my bare feet. I grew my beard to emphasize independence and the challenging of convention.

My assistant markets me using the brand. People remember both the look and the values it summarizes. When I speak at a conference now, people expect me to take off my shoes.

You probably won't want to go to the same lengths to establish your personal brand, not unless you work for yourself. But do think about your own strengths and how you can summarize them in a personal brand. Once you have done this, selling yourself becomes a lot, lot easier.

> 'YOUR PREMIUM BRAND HAD BETTER BE DELIVERING SOMETHING SPECIAL, OR IT'S NOT GOING TO GET THE BUSINESS.'
>
> WARREN BUFFETT

! Think profile

The more visual your personal brand, the easier it will be for people to remember.

Building your profile

Once you have a clear idea of your brand, you can begin to build your profile in a more focused way. There are simply not enough hours in the day to be all things to all people. In fact, if you spread yourself too thinly, your brand will become diluted and confused.

You build your profile by becoming:

• better known by more people
• associated with more networks, groups or organizations
• more opinionated and outspoken on topics you know something about.

In short, the greater the awareness people have of you and your interests, the more likely they are to want to connect with you. The Internet makes it far easier today than it once was to build these connections, join special interest groups and comment.

But equally important are those stronger 'face-to-face' relationships we develop. You may remember from Chapter 7 how important non-verbal communication is to our understanding of one other. So to build your profile you need to blend face-to-face with online activity.

As this part of the book is all about selling yourself, you may be hoping that it can help you progress your career. Indeed, even if you are not looking for a new job, being invited to consider one can be very flattering. Especially flattering is when you receive a surprise call or email from a head-hunter. Here are a few ways to make it easier for a head-hunter to find you:

- have an up-to-date LinkedIn profile with plenty of connections
- be good at what you do and have others in your business sector recognize that
- comment on the hot topics of the day in the trade press and online
- impress the people with whom you deal outside your own organization
- attend and, if possible, speak (even if only to ask a question) at industry events
- enter awards programmes where your achievements can be publicly recognized.

The final, simplest but not most obvious way to be spotted by head-hunters is to join their list of candidates. Most will allow you to upload your CV to their systems. Most will check new vacancies against their candidate database first, before looking further afield. All will respect the need for confidentiality and there's no shame in saying, 'Not now', if you are approached at a time you're not interested.

Strong and weak ties

Social scientists define the people we know as either strong or weak ties. Our strong ties are the people we know best and are closest to. These will include immediate family, close friends and colleagues. Our strong ties are the people we tend to spend the most time with.

Weak ties are those we know less well, perhaps only through someone we're closer to, often a strong tie. Examples of weak ties might be your partner's family, people living on your street and people who work at the same firm but with whom you do not have day-to-day contact.

It is usually true that you have more in common with your strong ties, but, because of this, you learn less that is new from them. Your weaker ties, with whom you have less in common, can be valuable sources of new knowledge and ideas. That's quite literally because they move in different circles from you and know well many people you don't know at all.

To build your profile, you need to make a conscious effort to spend time growing and cultivating your network of loose ties. What's more, connecting them with each other, perhaps introducing them when you discover they have common interests, will strengthen your network and sphere of influence. Remember that, to your weak ties, you are also a weak tie. By introducing them to new people, they are more likely to do the same for you.

Interestingly, it is considered impossible to grow your number of strong ties beyond around 150 people. That's because we don't have the mental (cognitive) capacity to maintain an unlimited number of contacts. This is called the 'Dunbar Number', after Robin Dunbar, the scientist who developed the theory.

If this really interests you, you can find many articles about it online. For now it's perhaps most important to remember the following:

• It pays to keep in touch with the people on the edges of your social and professional circles because they have the most potential to introduce you to totally new opportunities.

• It's human nature to talk most to those you know best, so a conscious effort is required to make time for those you know less well (your weak ties).

• You can't know everyone well, so as new strong ties are forged, others will inevitably slip further away (which happens naturally as our interests change over time).

The good news is that social media, particularly Twitter, make it far easier than ever before to maintain contact with your weak ties.

> **! Think profile**
>
> Often, the people who can help you the most are those who know you the least well.

Social media

For most people, social media is the best way to build and maintain profile. The Internet allows you to conveniently and effectively build and influence networks of contacts. It enables you to maintain contact with those you are closest to (your strong ties), even when you are geographically separated. Perhaps more useful from a selling perspective is the way social media can enable you to maintain contact with a large number of acquaintances (your loose ties).

There are many social media platforms you can use. The three most commonly used to build personal profile, and thus sell yourself, are Facebook, Twitter and LinkedIn. Each has a separate role to play:

Facebook	Twitter	LinkedIn
The most personal	The most far-reaching	The most professional
About what you do	About what you think	About what you know
Best for keeping in touch with strong ties	Best for recruiting/ managing weak ties	Best for managing/recruiting professional weak ties

Let's take a look at each of these social-media platforms in turn.

Facebook

It may not be politically correct but, when shortlisting candidates for a job interview, many people check out Facebook profiles. Most will recognize that a full and hectic social life is a healthy balance to a busy, focused work life. But do bear in mind when posting on Facebook that people might by assessing your suitability for a job by what you post.

On the other hand, as you get to know people better, connecting with them on Facebook enables you to strengthen the relationship. Facebook enables you to socialize with people without necessarily meeting them face to face. This breaks down geographic barriers, as well as being very time efficient. (However, it would be sad if you only socialized online.)

Of course, you can filter access to your Facebook profile using the privacy settings within the application. Better perhaps to show you have nothing to hide and think before posting anything particularly controversial or outrageous. Sometimes, it's better to 'bite your tongue' than make yourself unpopular.

There are a number of specific ways Facebook can help you build your personal profile. These include:

- making sure that your contact details and links to any blogs you write appear on your profile
- liking pages and joining groups that illustrate your range of interests (this might impress a recruiter)
- encouraging others to 'share' your post on their 'timeline' when you have a specific request connected with your career or work goals
- setting up a special-interest group or page – this positions you as someone willing to lead in a particular subject area (for example, there is a Facebook page for this book – www.facebook.com/salesfornonsalespeople).

'I AM ON FACEBOOK, BUT MAINLY AS A WAY TO SPY ON MY CHILDREN. I FIND OUT MORE ABOUT THEM FROM THEIR FACEBOOK PAGES THAN FROM WHAT THEY TELL ME.'

SALMAN RUSHDIE

! **Think profile**

Use Facebook to illustrate the good things about the way you live your life.

Twitter

Twitter is one of the most powerful tools you can use to promote yourself online. Positioned as a 'micro-blogging' platform, it enables you to maintain a low level of contact with a large number of people; in other words, to build and maintain your network of weak ties.

Twitter's strengths include:

- **brevity** – you have to summarize your point in 140 characters so you have to be clear and concise
- **links** – you can substitute some of those characters for links to websites or pictures
- **follow** – you can follow people you find interesting and see what they are tweeting
- **followers** – people who follow you form an instant audience for your tweets
- **retweets** – if your followers like what you have said, they can retweet it to their followers, who in turn might choose to follow you as well
- **hashtags** – using the # symbol, you can highlight a key word making it easier for others to find it; equally, you can identify others with similar interests and connect with them.

Your Twitter name, profile, photograph and web link are also very important, summarizing why you are interesting and worth following. Take time to make sure that your Twitter profile matches your personal brand.

To promote yourself on Twitter you need to be:

- **focused** – tweeting most often about the subjects relevant to your knowledge, experience and direction of career travel
- **spontaneous** – Twitter is an instant medium, so tweet when the thought strikes you or the topic is hot. Having Twitter on your phone makes this easy and using Tweet Deck on your laptop or PC means you can keep an eye on what those you follow are saying
- **proactive** – use hashtags to find out who's tweeting about your subject and join their debate.

An additional benefit of Twitter is that many journalists and media commentators use Twitter to research stories and identify people they can interview and quote. Following the journalists who write in your area of business means you will know when they ask for comment on a subject upon which you have something useful to say.

> `TWITTER IS MY BAR. I SIT AT THE COUNTER AND LISTEN TO THE CONVERSATIONS, STARTING OTHERS, FEELING THE ATMOSPHERE.`
>
> PAULO COELHO

> **! Think profile**
>
> Use Twitter to connect with people able to influence your future.

LinkedIn

LinkedIn can be summarized as a career-focused version of Facebook. It can also to a large extent form your CV. Your profile can list your educational achievements and career progress to date. You can also list your areas of interest, so that potential recruiters can see where your career might go next.

Important features of LinkedIn include:

- **testimonials** – you can encourage people who've worked with you to post testimonials on your profile
- **groups** – you can join special interest groups and debate with others who share your interests
- **network** – you can identify people able to influence your success and invite them to connect with you (ideally after having met or spoken with them already)
- **posts** – as with Facebook, you can post comments, thoughts and news about what you are doing (these will help people find you when they are searching for someone to help them with something you have expertise in)

- **contacts of contacts** – you can search the contacts of your direct connections and ask to be introduced to them. Perhaps more importantly, others can ask to be introduced to you.

If you become a serious user of LinkedIn, you can pay a modest subscription and gain the ability to:

- see who has viewed your profile – it's useful to know who's been checking you out
- directly contact people outside your immediate network using a feature called 'inmail'.

Finally, there are a number of programs such as HootSuite that can help you manage your social media activity. In particular, they enable you to post the same message on more than one platform simultaneously, as well as to schedule posts to go out later. These applications enable you to be active, without being overwhelmed.

'YOU CAN FOOL ALL THE PEOPLE SOME OF THE TIME, AND SOME OF THE PEOPLE ALL THE TIME, BUT YOU CANNOT FOOL ALL THE PEOPLE ALL THE TIME.'

ABRAHAM LINCOLN

> **!** **Think profile**
>
> Testimonials are really important, so make a point of asking those you impress the most to post a few words on your LinkedIn profile.

Blogging

An excellent way to build your profile is to blog. While you can set up your own blog, it can often be more effective to contribute regular, relevant content to existing blogs. As a rule of thumb, blogs should be:

- **short** – so that they are easy to read
- **topical** – expressing rational opinion about a current issue
- **credible** – because you have some knowledge or relevant experience.

Creating your own blog site will be most effective if:

- you are already a respected authority in your field
- you are confident you can maintain it with new content
- you believe your blog will attract visitors.

Contributing to popular blog websites, often run by business groups and publications, will work best for you if:

- you want to reach a wider audience faster than would be possible with your own site
- you want to debate as well as just comment
- there are already blog sites popular with the people you want to influence.

When writing your blog, or commenting on one written by someone else:

- be positive and suggest solutions rather than being negative or overly critical
- remember what you want the reader to 'know, think and do'
- focus on contributing to the debates most relevant to your personal goals.

Finally, a note of caution: not everybody who looks at your online profiles will be as nice a person as you are. Think twice before publishing your home address and invest in an effective spam filter. The downside of being easy to find is that you may be targeted by people trying to sell you things you don't want!

In this chapter you've discovered:

- the importance of personal brand
- the role of social media
- the value of maintaining regular contact with a wide circle of people.

9.

Networking – why you help yourself by helping others

Meeting new people

To succeed, we all need to keep meeting new people. That's because, over time, those we are currently close to will reduce in numbers. Some will move away, others will develop their interests in new directions that do not coincide with ours, and some inevitably will grow old and eventually die.

Equally, new people will move into your area, will become active in your profession or business sector, and reach a point where they could benefit from knowing you. If you don't go out of your way to meet new people, both you and they are missing out.

Networking is a generic term used to describe the process by which you meet and keep in touch with new people. More specifically, it is used to describe the way we do this by design, rather than chance. To go out networking is to go hunting for new contacts.

Chapter 4 of this book describes how you can attract and maintain someone's attention as part of the sales process. The purpose, then, is to start a conversation and establish sufficient rapport to lead the conversation towards a sale or decision. Networking is less about getting a sale and more about winning a friend.

Yet, paradoxically, many people find networking terrifying. It need not be so.

Why we network

To put it simply, we network to meet new people. That's because it's human nature to prefer to work or do business with people we know. It's also human nature to want to help others, which means we readily recommend people we know to others.

For example, if someone moves into your street and asks whether you know a good plumber, you will usually be more than happy to oblige. So imagine now that you're a cost accountant. Someone who knows you is asked whether they can recommend a potential new in-house accountant for a growing company. If they like you as a person and rate you as an accountant, they'll recommend you.

Networking is all about making it easier for people to recommend one another. It is not about selling directly to the person you've just met; that can be embarrassing as few people go to a networking event to buy. Most, in fact, go to sell.

Your objective has to be to encourage those you meet to refer you on. Encouraging people to refer you:

- enables you to gain something from meeting people not in a position to buy from you
- improves your success rate tenfold if the person you meet recommends you to ten people
- builds your network of 'weak ties' if you then use social media to keep in touch with them.

Don't worry that you will miss opportunities by not trying to sell when networking. If the person you are talking to is interested themselves, they will almost inevitably tell you.

> ! **Enjoy networking**
>
> Networking is about asking people to recommend us, not buy from us.

Talking to strangers

We can all find it difficult to start a conversation with someone we don't know. Even at a business or professional event where networking is expected, even the most confident networker can be overwhelmed by the challenge. This can be particularly true if the event is in an unfamiliar setting and not attended by anyone you know.

Even I was daunted when attending a reception and dinner at Buckingham Palace. When I entered the Picture Gallery where the reception was taking place, there were around 200 people, all, it seemed, deep in conversation.

I had two options: push into a conversation or stand on my own and feel very alone. I actually did neither of those, but instead walked slowly round the room admiring the amazing paintings that lined the gallery. As I passed round, I encountered others also admiring the art. It was easy to engage them in conversation about the picture we were both looking at. Once the ice was broken, we were away.

Here are three tips to help you feel comfortable talking to strangers:

1 Everyone goes to a networking event to network so is expecting to talk to strangers.

2 Remember that anyone else also on their own will probably be feeling just as anxious as you.

3 If you feel shy, say so – most people will respect your honesty and find you all the more interesting as a result.

Remember that people go to networking events to meet new people and discover new opportunities. People will buy you for who you are and what you can do for them. Your objective is to widen your network and increase your exposure to opportunity.

Over time, as confidence grows, most come to enjoy the discoveries that can only result from having a conversation with someone you don't know. Networking can be fun.

'FEAR MAKES STRANGERS OF PEOPLE WHO WOULD BE FRIENDS.'

SHIRLEY MACLAINE

> **!** **Enjoy networking**
>
> Think of networking as a human bran tub. You have to reach into the unknown to experience the joy of discovering something new.

Where to network

Almost any gathering provides an opportunity to network. Some obviously are more appropriate than others, but you should always be alert to an opportunity to meet and connect with someone new. Networking at social events can be useful, but business or professional events will increase your chances of meeting people able to help you.

Perhaps the best networking opportunities will be created if you attend:

• conferences attended by leaders in your field of business

• events attended by local business people

• fundraising events attended by the 'great and good'

• membership organization events (e.g. trade bodies and professional institutes).

For self-employed people, there are many organized breakfast networking clubs. These usually meet weekly and actively encourage members to pass one another sales leads. For some people, these work really well, for example financial advisers who rely on introductions to meet new clients.

It can also be useful to network on trains and planes. If you are going to sit facing someone for an hour or so, it makes sense to have a conversation with them. Just be sensitive to the fact that they are literally a captive audience.

Other places where you might meet people able to extend your network include:

• charities for whom you can volunteer or fundraise

• political parties and debating societies

• sports and social clubs.

'SUCCESSFUL PEOPLE ARE ALWAYS LOOKING FOR OPPORTUNITIES TO HELP OTHERS. UNSUCCESSFUL PEOPLE ARE ALWAYS ASKING, "WHAT'S IN IT FOR ME?"'

BRIAN TRACY

! Enjoy networking

The golden rule of networking is that, if you help others first, more will help you later. Build a reputation by knowing lots of useful people.

Your elevator pitch

Your elevator pitch is your verbal business card. It's the way you introduce yourself to others at a networking event. The elevator pitch is so called because it has to be very concise, short enough in fact to be delivered in a lift before the person you've bumped into gets out on the tenth floor.

As with so much of selling, your elevator pitch has to quickly and effectively communicate what you want the person you've just met to:

* **know** – about you and what you do
* **think** – how this might be useful to them or others in the future
* **do** – as a result of meeting you.

If you really do deliver your pitch in an elevator or lift, all you can realistically expect is for the chance meeting to end with a commitment to talk more another time. Swapping business cards and agreeing when you will ring them is perhaps all you can realistically achieve in the time you have.

More often than not, you deliver your elevator pitch by way of introduction, setting the scene for the conversation that follows. To do this, using the following structure might help you:

1 **Start with your name – and repeat it again at the end of your pitch.** If someone's listening carefully to what you say, they may well forget your name before you finish. Saying it at both start and finish makes it easy for them to pick up the conversation with a question.

2 **Say what you do.** For many people, this is surprisingly difficult to do. That's because they describe their role in too much detail. Just say what you do and keep it simple.

3 **Describe why you're different.** This is really important because it is where you differentiate yourself from others who do similar things. For example, if you work at a travel agency, you might specialize in Asia. If you are a manager in a large organization, you might also have an MBA or be a chartered manager.

4 **Explain what that means.** Imagine the other person butts in and says, 'So what?' This is your response, prepared and presented before they have the opportunity. So the travel agent specializing in Asia might say, 'This means I get asked to speak about travel at events and that generates lots of business for the firm I work for.'

5 **Say what you are looking for.** Always end with a request for help that is realistic and not a direct sales pitch to the person you're talking to. Our travel agent might say, 'I'm looking for more groups to talk to about Asia and don't mind speaking at short notice.'

Notice how the last point contains a benefit. The travel agent is willing to talk at short notice. This means that, when people hear of a speaker having to cancel somewhere, they will be more likely to recommend you.

Here's an example:

> *Hi, my name's Robert Ashton.*
>
> *I'm a successful social entrepreneur and bestselling author.*
>
> *My book on selling is aimed at people who want the skill, but not necessarily a sales career.*
>
> *That means that it helps the reader to sell themselves and succeed at work, as well as sell products and services.*
>
> *I'll also run 'selling for non-salespeople' workshops and am looking for groups of people who want to learn how to be more persuasive, without being pushy.*

Again, I've added a benefit at the end. My guess is that you, and those you might recommend me to as a workshop presenter, will want to be more persuasive without becoming pushy.

! Enjoy networking

If you can use humour or wordplay in your elevator pitch, you will be all the more memorable.

Being approachable

So far, we've talked about how to break the ice and start conversations. But networking is a two-way thing and you also want other people to feel comfortable approaching you. You also want them to find you easy to talk with. Being approachable will also take you a step closer to being popular.

People will be more likely to come up and talk to you at a networking event if you look:

- **happy** – with open body language, rather than looking nervous and standing with folded arms
- **smart** – well groomed and not dressed too outlandishly or weirdly
- **sober** – because nobody volunteers to be cornered by a drunk.

It can also help to position yourself in the room where people first arrive. Most people walk into a crowded room, stop and look around. Make eye contact and, unless they spot someone they know, they may well come over and talk to you. Remember that nobody likes to be on their own in a crowded room. They'll use you as a springboard to get deeper into the event.

Lastly, as your networking confidence grows, you will find the need to move on from people. When you're new to networking events, it can be both convenient and comfortable to spend the evening talking to just one friendly person. Later, you will want to 'work the room' so that you get the most from the event.

To politely park someone and move on to talk to someone else you can:

- introduce them to someone you've already spoken with and then excuse yourself quickly
- explain that you've just seen someone you really must talk to and promise to talk again soon.

If they really don't get the message that you need to move on, gently touching their arm as you explain the need to move on usually helps.

Being memorable

It is most important to be memorable for what you say, rather than for what you do or how you look. It might be amusing to spend the evening juggling with fruit from the buffet table, but while you might win a round of applause, you probably won't make many new contacts.

Much depends on the business sector you work in, your age, gender and where you are in your career. As a rule of thumb, though, people will find you easier to remember if you are:

- **positive and upbeat** – seeing the bright side rather than complaining about your problems
- **a little different** – perhaps dressed a little more individually than everyone else
- **physically different** – making the most of being very tall, short or perhaps a different colour from most people in the room.

For example, Wilfred Emmanuel-Jones was born in Jamaica and arrived in the UK with his parents as a small child. His lifetime ambition was be become a farmer. He has developed his own food brand 'The Black Farmer' and speaks to audiences about how he worked hard to realize his ambition. He uses his ethnicity to advantage, being memorable as one of very few black British farmers.

> **!** **Enjoy networking**
>
> Be yourself, be different and be remembered for what you stand for.

Speed networking

A good way to build your networking skill and practise your elevator pitch is to take part in a speed networking event. While it might sound daunting, in fact speed networking is a great way to make sure that you talk to everyone in the room. There is no ice to break, no risk of getting stuck with a bore and every opportunity you'll leave with a bunch of new, useful contacts.

Speed networking, as the name suggests, involves everyone in the room being divided into two groups. Often, there will be two rows of seats facing each other. You sit down and spend a minute or two introducing yourself to the person facing you. They then do the same. A facilitator with a stopwatch and whistle will keep you to time. After a fixed time, the members of one group move along one chair and the process is repeated.

Speed networking is particularly useful when you want to encourage dialogue between two quite different groups of people. For example, Council members and local residents, or people from two firms that are to work in partnership together. Here it forces people to talk to people they don't already know or work with.

In this chapter you've discovered:

- the importance of meeting new people
- how to become more confident starting conversations
- why it's so important to have and practise an elevator pitch.

10.

Job interviews – appearing confident, assertive and right for the job

Selling yourself

Applying for a new job is one of the most important sales tasks you can undertake. It's also one of the most difficult as you are the product and therefore will find it difficult to be objective. But the more objective and realistic you can be, the more mature and employable you will appear.

A good starting point is to reflect on your decision to find new work. This is as true if you are seeking promotion or looking to change to a new employer. In short, are you looking to progress to something better, or to escape from somewhere you no longer feel comfortable? You need to be sure of your motives if you are to be successful.

Here are some common reasons people cite for wanting to change their job:

• the work no longer interests you and you have become bored

• you feel undervalued, overlooked and taken for granted

• you feel insecure as the organization is not doing so well these days

• you don't get on with the people you work with, especially your boss.

Sometimes, of course, the best course of action is to become more proactive and resell yourself to your current employer. This is covered in the next section of the book, Chapters 11–15. For now, though, let's assume that you're confident that your best course of action is to sell yourself to a new employer.

SWOT

A good way to prepare to apply for a new job is to take a long, hard look at what you enjoy and do well. It's also good to be realistic about what you don't enjoy or find easy. Perhaps the best way to do this is to carry out a self-SWOT analysis.

SWOT is an acronym and stands for:

- **S**trengths – the things you know and do (and have done) well
- **W**eaknesses – the things you're not so good at or perhaps have little experience of
- **O**pportunities – the things you think your experience, knowledge, skills and connections will enable you to do best
- **T**hreats – the things you feel could trip you up, for example not having completed the professional exams or being reliant on public transport to get to work.

Completing a self-SWOT will help you select the best jobs to go for. It will also help you focus your application and CV to highlight your relevant strengths.

It's also useful to think about your strengths in terms of features and benefits. This will help you sell yourself at interview. In this context, features are what you are good at and the benefits, what those features mean to your prospective employer.

For example:

Feature	Benefit
You have a food hygiene certificate.	Flexible – you can help out in the café from day one.
You represent your current firm on a trade body.	Connected – you bring a reputation and contacts.
You live five minutes from the office.	Weatherproof – you'll always be able to get in.
You worked in a similar firm in a different country.	You both know the ropes and may bring new ideas.

Note that it's not always the obvious benefits that will appeal most to a new boss. For example, the boss might be fed up with having to cope with people unable to get in when the weather is bad. The fact that you live five minutes away might be more important to her than a rival candidate having more qualifications. Remember that buying decisions are usually emotionally driven.

'LIFE ISN'T ABOUT FINDING YOURSELF. LIFE IS ABOUT CREATING YOURSELF.'

GEORGE BERNARD SHAW

Your CV

A CV is a selling document and should be tailored to emphasize the benefits you would bring to the advertised vacancy. There is no shortage of advice on CV writing, so perhaps the greatest challenge you face is choosing which piece of advice to follow.

If you've ever recruited or shortlisted for interview, you'll know just how little time is spent sorting a pile of applications from the 'maybe' pile to the 'definitely not' pile. It's a harsh process, often completed at speed and, in my experience, often in the evening after a long day at the office.

What this means is that your application has to stand out from the crowd and clearly illustrate why you're worth meeting. And this has to be achieved in seconds because, unless the top of page one grabs attention, the rest will probably never get read.

That's not to say that recruiters are unfair or fail to recognize the need to avoid discriminating unfairly; it's more that, if a CV doesn't sell you at first glance, it won't sell you at all. Here then are some tips to help you make sure your CV sells you. Your CV must be:

- **easy to read** – that means 12-point type, short sentences, lots of bullet points and no acronyms or jargon

- **first person** – make it you speaking from the page (use 'I have', rather than the third person 'she has')

- **upbeat** – positive and explaining the benefits you bring

- **illustrated** – with a professionally taken 'business-like' photo of you in the top right-hand corner

- **accurate** – with no typos or grammatical errors

- **punchy** – opening with a paragraph that explains exactly why you're the person for the job

- **short** – no more than two pages of A4

- **connected** – list your social-media profiles and add hyperlinks.

It is also useful to use some of the key words on the job ad in your application. This is a sales technique called 'mirroring'. By repeating some of the recruiter's key words your CV will resonate with the reader. 'She's using my words,' his subconscious will say, 'so she must therefore be on my wavelength.' For example:

- **Ad says:** 'Must have good working knowledge of Photoshop'
- **CV says:** 'I have a good working knowledge of Photoshop'
- **CV should not say:** 'Excellent Photoshop skills'.

Your covering letter or email should also confront and overcome the likely barriers that might exclude you from the shortlist. This shows that you're thinking from the employer's perspective and not just your own. For example:

- 'Although I live 20 miles from your office, my grandmother's house is nearby and I plan to sleep there when I work late or if the weather is bad.'
- 'The good news about my disability is that it doesn't affect my work and you will qualify for a grant to adapt my workstation.'

Mirroring also works well in an interview, where you can repeat key words from questions in your answers. You can also mirror body language, for example lean forward when the other person leans forward.

! Get hired

Life is like physics. For every disadvantage there is an equal and opposite advantage. All you have to do is find and highlight it!

Getting shortlisted

Large organizations have very structured recruitment procedures. You need to follow these diligently because to deviate from them could disqualify you. However, small organizations will be less formal and may be influenced by some pre-shortlisting sales effort on your part.

Choosing to influence the shortlisting process has to be your decision alone. It can work against as well as for you. But, if you feel you are likely not to be shortlisted, perhaps because of poor exam results or a missing 'essential' qualification, you probably have little to lose.

Key to success is for the recruiter to recognize that you're taking an enthusiastic interest in the organization. You need to do this in a measured and subtle way. You don't want to appear to be stalking the person you hope will be your next boss. Timing is everything, as your activity needs to coincide with the shortlisting process.

Here are three ways you can make a name for yourself, before being shortlisted:

1 **Look for LinkedIn connections** – you're applying to a small firm and so probably know the boss's name. Look them up on LinkedIn and see whether you have any common contacts. Mention to those you think might recommend you that you've applied for a job with XYZ. Encourage them to 'put in a good word' for you. This will show that you are well networked.

2 **Follow the boss on Twitter** – not only will this show that you're taking an interest, but it will generate an email to say that you're now following. Make sure that your profile and most recent ten tweets are appropriate to the job you're applying for. Retweet them sparingly and, most importantly, don't 'unfollow' them if not shortlisted. They might still come back to you if the first batch proves unsuitable.

3 **Mystery shop** – if the business has a retail outlet, or you know who some of its customers are, pop along and check them out. Mention your name and that you've just applied for a job. Say you hope to get shortlisted.

To help you decide where to draw the line, here are three things you should probably not do:

1 **Befriend them on Facebook** – that would be too intrusive and be the digital equivalent of standing too close and invading their personal space.

2 **Go out of your way to meet them at a networking event** – again, this is too 'full on' and potentially very embarrassing.

3 **Write an over-the-top application** – if you spend all weekend on a lavish, detailed application containing much more information than is required, it will look as if you are desperate.

And, finally, remember that business communities can be very small, with everybody knowing everybody else. This means that, even if not shortlisted for the job you've applied for, if you make a favourable impression, you might well get passed on to someone else also looking to recruit. A surprising number of jobs are never advertised but are just filled by the recruiter asking around for recommendations.

> **!** **Get hired**
>
> Bend the rules but don't break the opportunity.

Arriving at the interview

As with any selling situation, it's the preparation that makes the difference. You've thought hard and applied for all the right reasons. Your CV and covering email or letter were carefully crafted to show how perfectly your skills and experience fit the role. Perhaps you're already following your prospective boss on Twitter and have an understanding of her attitudes and priorities. You've arrived early and are waiting to be seen. My bet is that you will be getting pretty nervous.

The interview is the climax of what has often been a long and arduous journey. But being nervous will not improve your performance. So, before you arrive, try to do all or some of these:

- Read through your application and any background data on the organization and role.
- Google to see whether there's any breaking news you can ask about to break the ice.
- Think about the questions you least hope you will be asked and have answers ready.
- Be punctual and allow time for a coffee and/or relaxing walk before the meeting.
- Visit the toilet when you arrive to check your hair (and make-up).
- Be nice to the person who checks you in at reception; they may well be asked for their feedback as part of the selection process.

- The more confident you can appear and feel when you arrive, the better the interview is likely to go.

> **! Get hired**
>
> Don't worry about what you don't know; it's OK for you to ask questions in an interview, too.

Questions and answers

If you've applied for several jobs recently, you may well have more interview experience than the person sitting across the table. Small firms in particular will often recruit informally, hiring family and friends of friends. Be prepared to be proactive and make it as easy as you can for the interviewer.

Perhaps the most important thing to remember in an interview is to be you. Don't try to be what you think the interviewer wants you to be. Even if you can pull it off, you won't be able to maintain the pretence once hired. Just be yourself and let the interviewer see that you are comfortable with yourself.

That said, don't go out of your way to highlight or even exaggerate anything that sets you apart from the majority. Most people are fairly relaxed and tolerant, but they will feel uncomfortable if you are too overt. You're not there to campaign for equality but to get a job.

The principal difference between a job interview and almost any other sales meeting is that the buyer asks most of the questions. You've already made your written pitch and been shortlisted. A job interview gives the recruiter the opportunity to:

- check out some of the detail behind your CV
- see how articulate, able and enthusiastic you are
- judge how well you will fit in with the team.

However professional the process, much of the decision-making process will be based on intuition. In other words, how they feel about you will be as important as what they find out about you. So it's very important to be relaxed yourself, as this will both relax the interviewer and allow your personality to shine through.

All of the questioning techniques introduced in Chapter 3 apply in a job interview. Remember to:

- answer open questions simply and clearly, without rambling or contradicting yourself
- answer closed questions decisively and confidently
- keep in mind the biggest benefits you feel you offer the employer and refer to them more than once
- ask for clarification if you are not sure what the questioner is really wanting to know
- repeat key words from the question in your answers
- be modest and attribute some of your success to those around you – this shows you're a team player
- maintain eye contact when answering – to glance away can appear insincere
- smile and, if confident enough, use humour to defuse any tension that might develop.

Expect to be asked questions about:

- your current employer to see how well you understand the business – but do remember to refuse to answer questions that might betray commercial confidences
- the extent to which you have autonomy and authority over decision making
- your reasons for wanting the job (don't say: because it pays better than my current job)
- why you are planning to leave your current job
- how you would go about the job if appointed.

Remember, too, that you may well be asked questions to explore how well you would fit in with the existing team. This is vitally important if you'll be reporting directly to the owner of a small business. There are no right or wrong answers, but do suggest that you can be flexible and adapt. For example, it's good to get across that:

- you work well under pressure but can also find plenty to do when things are quiet
- you can work in a team and think for yourself, too
- you understand risk and, while willing to make decisions, are not prone to being rash.

As with any sales interview, if you overstate your ability, or exaggerate your achievements or capabilities, it will inevitably show. It's actually very difficult to deviate too far from the truth without the other person spotting it.

! Get hired

Remember that the interviewer might actually be more desperate to fill a vacancy than you are to take the job. It's OK to question the deal you're offered and negotiate a little.

Interview panels

Usually, you are interviewed by one or two people. In a large organization, they will have a list of prepared questions to ask you. Each candidate will be asked the same questions and the answers each gives will be scored. The score for each candidate creates a useful starting point for the discussion about whom, if anyone, to appoint.

In this situation, you will naturally pay equal attention to each interviewer. But what happens when you find yourself facing a panel of six or even more interviewers? It becomes far more difficult to pay attention to everyone, especially the quiet guy at the end who says nothing and just makes notes.

Selling yourself to a group is always harder than being interviewed by one or two people. A formal interview by panel can be particularly daunting as they will almost inevitably be lined up on the opposite side of the table. Here are some tips to help you handle an interview panel:

- Smile and nod at each of the interviewers as they introduce themselves.
- If they don't introduce themselves, ask them to do so, as they've probably forgotten.
- When answering questions, make sure that you glance at everyone, not just the person who asked it.
- Not all panel members will find every question relevant to them, so don't be surprised if some look disinterested – it's not you!
- It's not unusual for panel members to disagree with one other – be diplomatic and don't take sides.

Sometimes, when facing an interview panel, you can get the feeling you've lost one of the members. Their body language or sudden interest in their phone will tell you they've reached a conclusion. If you feel confident enough, ask why when your opportunity to ask questions arrives.

Go back to the subject being discussed when their body language changed. Say something like: 'I'm not sure that I explained myself clearly enough when we were talking about xyz. Could I just check that you got my point that xyz ...?' Look straight at the person you're worried about so that they feel obliged to answer.

This will force them either to reassure you or to tell you what's on their mind. If you ask in a non-aggressive way, they'll probably explain why they're not certain. Then you can deal with it. This is no different from dealing with an objection when trying to close a sale. It's just that you are selling yourself.

Trial by sherry

Charities often use this technique to allow trustees to vet candidates for senior posts. It usually takes place before the interviews and consists of a lunchtime or evening reception at which candidates, trustees and usually the senior team mingle over food and drinks.

Schools often use a variation of this where candidates are shown round. How well they respond to, and impress, those they meet will be fed back to the interview panel. Many candidates find it useful to meet the organization's wider community before the interview. It helps them understand something of the culture and, of course, they get to meet those who hold the power.

If you find yourself invited to a 'meet the Board' or similar, here are some things to bear in mind:

- Do your research first and know a little about as many as possible of the people you're going to meet.
- If someone you know will be there has achieved great things, be sure to flatter them just a little by saying how impressed you are. However, don't overdo this.
- Err on the side of modesty when deciding what to wear – be you, but don't be controversial.
- Be positive about those you work with now and have worked with in the past. It's a small world and, even if the person you're talking to doesn't like your current boss, they will think more of you if you are tactful and don't run anyone down.
- Lastly, not everyone's opinion will be taken seriously. Every group has at least one 'difficult person' who will disagree for all the wrong reasons. So all may not be lost if you find yourself cornered by someone who's opinion of you appears to be unfairly biased.

Assessment centres

Organizations that take on a lot of new recruits, particularly graduates, often use assessment centres to help them select the best candidates. The good thing about this is that you have plenty of opportunity to show what you are capable of. Assessment centres vary considerably, depending on the job. While you might find the concept daunting, remember that they provide you with more opportunity to shine. Assessment centres give recruiters an opportunity to really get to know you.

The interview result

If you are successful and decide to accept the job, make sure that you leave your old place on good terms. Do not treat your notice period as an opportunity to say all the things you've been holding back for years.

Instead, make sure you leave on good terms and use social media to keep in touch with people. There's a surprisingly good chance you'll work with, or do business with, your former colleagues in the future, so you need to remain on good terms.

If you are not successful, ask yourself these three questions:

1 Was this really the right job for me?
2 What can I learn from the process and how will I apply it next time?
3 Are these people I would really like to work with and so how can I keep in touch?

'CHOOSE A JOB YOU LOVE, AND YOU WILL NEVER HAVE TO WORK A DAY IN YOUR LIFE.'

CONFUCIUS

> ! **Get hired**
>
> 'No' need not mean 'never'; it just means 'not right now'. Never lose touch with those you want to work with in the future.

In this chapter you've discovered:

- that the better you know yourself, the easier it will be to sell yourself
- that you can do much more to influence your success than send a CV and wait
- that a job interview is a sales meeting that should lead to a negotiation.

PART III

Selling to colleagues

11.

Managing your career – take control of your future

Take time to reflect

In 1983 I was recently married yet spent six months living away from home during the week because I had applied for and won promotion at work. Worse, my reward for abandoning my new wife for four nights a week was just a £1,500-a-year pay rise and a higher-spec Ford Sierra.

Within a year of moving house, to a place where neither of us felt at home, four hours' drive from my wife's family, our first child was born. The next promotion opportunity arose and once more, I found myself working away for much of the week.

In the eyes of my sales director, I was a rising star. Looking back, I would say I was a fool. Fortunately, I am still married to my wife and my children have grown up to be balanced, objective and successful on their own terms. I made the classic mistake of chasing the opportunities others dangled in front of me, rather than working out what was best for me, and, of course, my new family.

Even today, when it's far more common for people to move between organizations, the expectation remains that you will apply for promotion because it suits your employer. Too often we do as suggested, because to turn down the 'opportunity' risks our being written off as unambitious and never asked again.

The truth, however, is that you need to take control of your career. You need a clear vision of where you want to go and to accept that, as age and circumstances change, so, too, will your vision for the future. In short, you need to be proactive and sell yourself, your vision and the benefits that will accrue to your boss, colleagues and whole organization if you are allowed to follow your own path.

'A CAREER IS WONDERFUL, BUT YOU CAN'T CURL UP WITH IT ON A COLD NIGHT.'

MARILYN MONROE

Career plan

Chapter 6 introduced you to Maslow's hierarchy of needs. You may remember that his theory suggests that, until you've got the basics such as food and shelter covered, you won't worry too much about realizing your dreams. What this means in terms of career planning is this: you will be far less fussy when looking for your first job than you will when looking for a career move 20 years later.

That's because, when you start out, you may have qualifications and some work experience but no track record. As time goes by, you build experience, reputation and a network of contacts. These make it easier to change jobs. But, equally, you can become very familiar and comfortable with an organization and become reluctant to venture outside to somewhere where everything will be new.

This means that, if you are good at what you do and don't encounter any major setbacks, your range of options widens as you grow older. In fact, as you start to approach retirement age, you may find you need less income. This presents even more opportunities. In fact, it's not unusual for people to 'drop out' of high-pressure jobs in their fifties to do something simpler and rewarding in other ways.

Here are some pointers to help you create a career plan:

- **Where are you now?** – be honest with yourself about how you arrived in the job you have now. List what you like most and least, then ask yourself why. Understand the value of your experience and skills to date. This is your starting point.

- **Where do I want to be in ten years' time?** – this could be the career-specific goals you considered when reading Chapter 6. If not, think about them now. What do you think your priorities will be in ten years' time and what job is most likely to deliver them? This should not be based on any established career track your organization might have. It needs to be about you.

- **Define the gap** – what are the skills, qualifications and experiences you need to start having now, to bridge the gap and find yourself where you want to be in the future?
- **Write it down** – there's no substitute for a written plan. Once you've written it down, perhaps in two-year steps, the transition should look far more achievable.
- **Do it!** – don't just file the plan away. Make a diary note to review monthly and add to the plan your achievements as you make them. If you make a list and tick things off as you do them, you will be able quickly see the progress you are making.

Once you have a career plan, you can start to enlist the support of the people you work with to achieve it. It's important to aim to do this as collaboratively as you can. You will inevitably find yourself in competitive situations at times. However, being clear about what you want and why will make you more focused and therefore only compete when necessary.

> I WAS NOT ENCOURAGED TO FOLLOW THE CAREER OF A WRITER BECAUSE MY PARENTS THOUGHT THAT I WAS GOING TO STARVE TO DEATH. THEY THOUGHT NOBODY CAN MAKE A LIVING FROM BEING A WRITER IN BRAZIL.
>
> PAULO COELHO

! Steer your career

Your career plan will deliver the fuel you need to realize your life plan.

Positioning

The last part of this book helped you develop some of the techniques you need to become more positive, assertive and better connected. Now we need to think far more about how you fit within your team and organization. That's because, to get on within an organization, or even to leave it on good terms, you need to manage the way others will react or be affected by your actions.

A good way to think about this is to consider yourself as a product and your organization your marketplace. Where a product fits in a marketplace is called its 'position'. Marketers work to influence perceptions of price, value and their product's physical characteristics to more clearly define, or indeed change, its position.

A great example is the soft drink Lucozade. When I was a child, it came in a glass bottle covered in crinkly orange cellophane. The marketing strapline was: 'Lucozade aids recovery.' It was sold as an energy booster for sick children.

Today, children are sick far less often and parents are less inclined to give them a brightly coloured sugary drink when they are unwell. The marketers predicted this decline in demand. They also saw the gyms and running growing in popularity and so repositioned Lucozade as a sports drink.

One of the tough questions you need to ask yourself is this: is the demand for what I do growing or in decline? Clearly, if it's in decline, you may need to think long and hard about developing new skills, or, like Lucozade, finding new ways to utilize your existing skills.

A good way to find out how you are currently positioned in your workplace is to ask others to describe you. In fact, if your organization uses 360-degree appraisal processes, you may already know. If not, ask someone you trust to do an informal survey to find out how you are perceived.

Sometimes, the truths that this process reveals are a little painful. But it's important to recognize that, only when you know how others see you, can you start to influence their perception.

Your career plan will help you understand where you need to position yourself. For example, if you work in IT support and see the future in social media, you might decide to:

• adopt a more trendy haircut and style of dress

• invest more time in building your own social-media profile

• find some courses that can help you develop your social-media skills

• talk to your internal IT support client about social media and let them spread word of your developing interest.

Once your reputation as a social-media guru starts to emerge, you may find that you can create a new opportunity. You could do some research and show how creating an internal social-media agency could save your employer money and boost the bottom line. You have then created yourself a new role.

What is equally important is that you have created a new future for yourself in a way that helps those around you do better, too. It is always more rewarding to create a new job than compete with others for a promotion you may not really want.

'I'M NOT INTERESTED IN PEOPLE POSITIONING ME NEXT TO OTHER ARTISTS.'

LADY GAGA

! Steer your career

A career is like a bottle of Lucozade, better if positioned to appeal to as wide an audience as possible.

Getting trained

It could be that you work for an organization that does formal appraisals and training needs analysis and, most importantly, has a training budget. But it's equally likely that you do not. And, even if you do, how do you sell the idea of you going to that important conference or attending a course for which there is no budget?

You've worked out that to get on you need those additional skills and so, to you, the training is important. You need to sell the benefits of attending to your boss, or perhaps someone in the HR department.

The first barrier you may encounter is that it was your idea, not theirs. People are always more committed to their own ideas than other people's. So, if you've yet to identify the course you need, discussing it with your boss now might be a good idea. It gives her the opportunity to find and recommend something. If she does this, she has automatically committed to finding a way to pay for it.

Here are some tips to help you persuade your employer to pay for your training or conference place:

- **Features and benefits** – be analytical about what new skills the course will bring to your company and what those benefits are worth. Remember that there will be both hard and soft benefits:
  - ° *hard benefits* can be quantified in monetary terms – you gain a Health & Safety qualification and your company saves on external consultancy fees
  - ° *soft benefits* are harder to quantify but no less real all the same – you attend a conference and might meet a number of potential new clients for your company.
- **Offer to contribute** – show your commitment by offering to take the time as holiday. In other words, you give your time and the firm gives the money. This is called negotiating, where both sides give something.
- **Overcome objections** – remember that 'no' rarely means 'never'. Find out what the barrier is and promise to go and find a way around it. If it's just money, show how the cost can be covered by savings you can identify elsewhere. Be creative, positive and just a little persistent.
- **Close the deal** – too often, we put off asking outright because we fear that the answer will be 'no', or that we will somehow offend by being forthright. Ask, and keep on asking!

Finally, if you really want to do the course and your company won't pay, remember that it's often possible to take out career development loans to spread the cost. If you want to do something badly enough, and are convinced it will boost your career, you sometimes have to be brave and pay for it yourself.

'IT'S ALL TO DO WITH THE TRAINING: YOU CAN DO A LOT IF YOU'RE PROPERLY TRAINED.'

QUEEN ELIZABETH II

! Steer your career

Don't just ask for what you want, negotiate for what you want.

Sabbaticals and secondments

As your focus improves and your selling skills develop, you can sometimes feel the need to escape the routine and really think about your future. Of course, a good holiday can take you some of the way, but now and again it's good to take a break from the day-to-day work and do something completely different.

Many people take a gap year before going to university. A few take a gap year later in life as they prepare for retirement. But too few take any significant time out in between – well, apart from career breaks to raise children, and few would say they provide much opportunity to think.

Sabbaticals are a complete break from work, with the ability to return to your job when you return. They can give you the opportunity to:

• travel and see more of the world

• volunteer locally and see life from a completely different perspective

• deal with a family crisis such as a very sick parent.

Sabbaticals are usually unpaid, although your employer might pay you something, especially if you will be working part time or available to answer any queries.

Secondments are more work-related and might enable you to:

• work for a while with one of your company's customers or suppliers to widen your industry experience

• see how organizations like yours work in other countries

• complete a qualification such as an MBA.

Secondments are usually paid.

Both sabbaticals and secondments can develop you as a person and enable you to return to work refreshed, energized and brimming with new ideas. Neither needs be for a full year. Many advocate six weeks as being long enough to acclimatize, make a difference for a month and then have some time off before returning to work.

You should sell the idea of a secondment or sabbatical in the same was as you sell the opportunity for you to have some training. After all, the benefits are broadly the same. Perhaps more so than with training, it pays to discuss the idea with your boss early. This gives them both an opportunity to help you shape the trip and time to get used to the idea.

Remember that, often, the biggest concern your boss will have is knowing how your workload will be covered while you're away. The more you can help with this, without committing anyone until you have agreement to go, the easier it will be to sell.

'WHAT DO WE LIVE FOR, IF IT IS NOT TO MAKE LIFE LESS DIFFICULT FOR EACH OTHER?'

GEORGE ELIOT

> **!** **Steer your career**
>
> The best way to see how others live is to go and live with them for a while.

Taking control

As with so much in life, you will get further if you take control and positively manage your career. Your boss, colleagues and everyone you encounter has a role to play, but only if you sell them the benefits of doing so.

Here are some final thoughts on how you might make it as easy as possible for others to help your career progress:

- Be open about your ambition, but be realistic, too, or people might think you arrogant.
- Help others with their careers, and others will be more likely to help you with yours.
- Focus people's attention on your strengths and your learning on your weaknesses.
- Cultivate and impress those able to make a difference to your success, perhaps by mentoring or simply opening the door to an otherwise hidden opportunity.
- Bounce back from the inevitable setbacks and avoid becoming bitter about what might appear to have been unfair decisions.

- Remember that, however much others can be encouraged to help you, at the end of the day you have to be the person trying hardest to grow your career.

'WHEN ONE DOOR CLOSES, ANOTHER OPENS; BUT WE OFTEN LOOK SO LONG AND SO REGRETFULLY UPON THE CLOSED DOOR THAT WE DO NOT SEE THE ONE WHICH HAS OPENED FOR US.'

ALEXANDER GRAHAM BELL

! Steer your career

You can't be a back-seat driver when it comes to navigating your career journey.

In this chapter you've discovered:

- the importance of having a clear career plan
- that finding out how others see you will help you define your market position
- how to sell your boss the idea of you going on the training courses that can make a real difference to your career.

12.
Becoming an authority – how to be a thought leader

Be the 'go to' person at work

In every firm, there's someone who seems to know all the answers. They've been around a while, seem to know lots of people and, more importantly, know how things work. It's rarely the most senior member of the team. More often, it's just someone who made it his or her business to find stuff out.

My wife is that person at the school where she works. She's the business manager and has been there more than 20 years. When anything breaks, she knows who to call to fix it. When something can't be found, she usually knows the best place to look. And when there's a crisis, she remembers how the problem was solved last time. Everyone seeks her advice. She is the 'go to' person.

Having the most local knowledge can make you hugely popular within your organization. But being considered an authority by those in your wider business sector will help you more. You see, when it comes down to getting on and climbing the career ladder, it's your credibility outside your organization that will get you taken seriously within your organization.

Of course, much depends on the size of the organization. My wife is an authority within the school where she works. But her school is one of more than 400 in the county and, at that higher level, she's not well known at all. If she was ambitious, which she is not, she would need to become an authority in her field, over as wide an area as possible.

What's more, when you start to look more widely than your immediate workplace, you need to become authoritative about bigger things. You need to be contributing to the debate, helping others form opinions and, at times, using your credibility to challenge the status quo and encourage innovation.

Being an authority is also very different from being given authority. In fact, you can be quite senior in the organizational hierarchy and have the authority to manage, delegate, spend money and make decisions, but still not be considered an authority in your field. You may well know people like this. Often, they've grown up with a business, but have a very narrow experience base. They have power, but not authority.

What is authority?

Dictionary definitions of authority include 'the power to influence others, especially because of one's commanding manner or one's recognized knowledge about something' and 'a person with extensive or specialized knowledge about a subject; an expert'. But perhaps the most revealing of all definitions is: 'the confidence resulting from personal expertise'.

You see, being authoritative is very good for self-confidence, and that will make people far more likely to buy from you. This is as true when you are selling products and services to customers as it is when you are selling ideas and projects within your organization. Becoming more authoritative will help you wherever your career takes you.

Things that will make you more authoritative include:

- **being an early adopter** – taking the time and trouble to explore and become comfortable with new ideas, technologies and techniques
- **reading around your subject** – knowing what's new and likely to impact on the work you do
- **having opinions** – and, most importantly, being able to back them up with reasoned argument
- **being known** – by the leaders in your field
- **willingly helping others** – because only by helping others do we grow ourselves.

Imagine for a moment that there are two colleagues doing similar jobs in a large organization. One – let's call him Tim – is eager, 'out there' and fast becoming an expert in his field. Tom, on the other hand, is quieter, focuses on getting the job done and prefers the tried-and-trusted route to the new. Tom is actually better at the job than Tim.

Now imagine that both Tim and Tom want to upgrade their computer system but the company has money to buy only one. They make similar budget proposals to their boss. Although Tom is the more competent, Tim gets the cash. Why? Well, because Tim is better known and their boss's boss thought he would 'make better use' of the investment.

This might sound unfair, but it's what happens in organizations. Both Tim and Tom had to sell the idea of being given faster IT. Tom, being better organized, probably wrote the better proposal. But it was Tim the big boss had heard good things about and so she suggested Tim wins.

Being viewed as authoritative makes you more likely to win and that is what selling is all about.

THE WISEST HAVE THE MOST AUTHORITY.'

PLATO

 Be an authority

You don't have to be the best person to succeed, just the best-known person capable of success.

Mentors

To become and remain a respected authority you need to push yourself. People will look to you for guidance and advice. In just the same way, you, too, will benefit from the support of someone more experienced. They do not need to work in the same line of business as you, but they do need to be respected authorities in their own field.

Just as top athletes have a coach to push them, so, too, will you perform better if you have someone coaching you. There are business and personal coaches out there. Many do an excellent job. But, more realistically, you are going to find a mentor.

You mentor could be:

- an older, more experienced colleague
- a leader in your field looking now to help others make their way
- someone who has volunteered for a mentoring programme.

As with any aspect of selling, you need to help a potential mentor see what the benefits are to them of helping you. They should never be financial, more the satisfaction of helping someone younger avoid pitfalls, identify opportunity, and recognize and develop talent.

A surprising number of quite influential people agree to be mentors. They have to believe you have ability, ambition and won't take too much of their time. For the mentor, helping someone grow their future can be a very rewarding reminder of just how far they themselves have come.

Furthermore, if you have the ear of a respected leader in your field, you will become someone others go to for advice – if only because they know you have someone you in turn can ask.

> **! Be an authority**
>
> Who you know can be more important than what you know.

Knowledge

To be an authority, you clearly have to know your stuff. But you certainly don't have to spend all your spare time reading academic papers, surveys and reports. What's important is to know enough of the 'big picture' to form a credible opinion. Then you can comment on the world in which you work, confident that you know where to look if asked for detail.

One of the problems of the modern age is the volume of knowledge at our fingertips. Google any subject, however niche, and you find vast amounts of knowledge. This can take the form of published research, case studies and reports.

Governments commission lots of research and base policy decisions upon it. Those working at grassroots level within those policy areas have to show how their project reflects the research findings. This can be daunting if you find yourself asked to write a funding bid.

The same will be true if you are making an internal bid for resources to develop a new area of your work. The more you can use existing knowledge to reassure people that there is little risk to what you are proposing, the more likely you will be to succeed. What's more, if you have a reputation for digging deep into your subject area, people will expect you to be proposing things that take the organization along the right track.

There are two kinds of knowledge:

1 **explicit** – factual, process and easy to write down and share
2 **tacit** – the product of experience and thus less easily defined and shared.

To be considered an authority, you need to have explicit knowledge but will be valued more for the tacit knowledge you have acquired over time. Paradoxically, it's the explicit knowledge that can take a long time to acquire. The tacit knowledge that people value most you tend to pick up as you go along.

Here are some short cuts to help you keep up to date with the developing explicit knowledge in your area of work:

- **Read reviews** – let others churn through all the data and read their summaries and interpretations.

- **Follow pundits** – use Twitter to follow opinion formers and spend your time exploring where they disagree, rather than agree, with each other (most tweet links to the reviews they write).

- **Set up Google alerts** – you can set up Google to search for new content in your field every day, then send you a list of summaries and hyperlinks.

- **Follow blogs** – some bloggers are very influential, so follow them but don't always agree with everything they write.

Innovate

People will always admire those who do the things they dare not do themselves. When you do something others consider risky and you succeed, they will almost inevitably say that they planned to do it, too, but that you beat them to it. What this really means is that they'd thought about it, but certainly not with any real commitment actually to doing it.

For example, I bought a derelict farmhouse and buildings then restored them to create some workspace and our family home. Once work started, many people stopped to tell me how they'd been planning to do the same here. However, when I bought the place, it had been on the market a while and attracted no offers. I paid a very low price and that, of course, mitigated the financial risk I was taking that others had feared.

If you are one of the first to try new technology, processes or work practices, you will find that others will be quick to ask you how you did it. Of course, you don't have to be the first in the world to try something new, just the first in your firm, or even department. Your regular trawling of emerging knowledge and comment will have tipped you off about what is perhaps already being done in a similar situation.

> 'BEING SECOND IS TO BE THE FIRST OF THE ONES WHO LOSE.'
>
> AYRTON SENNA

! Be an authority

It can be less risky to be one of the first than to be one of the many who follow later.

Lead opinions

The more you are viewed as someone who leads opinion, the more people will come to you for advice. The more they come to you for advice, the more seriously your ideas will be taken. The more seriously you are taken, the less hard you have to sell those ideas to others.

Becoming an opinion leader means being considered influential, and that means being outspoken. It's not necessary to write long and detailed blogs (see Chapter 8). Those with the most influence themselves will have little time to read long articles. They prefer 'soundbites', one-liners and short pieces that capture the moment and present it from a different perspective.

After the war the British Prime Minister Winston Churchill used the phrase 'iron curtain' a number of times in speeches in the late 1940s. He was referring to concerns that Russia would place an impenetrable shield around the countries it controlled. He was not the first to use the phrase but he is remembered for bringing it into the everyday language of the time. It became a very convenient way to describe what in reality was a complex combination of political, trade and physical barriers between Eastern and Western Europe.

When writing comments and to a certain extent blogs, using fewer words will usually deliver a greater impact. The only exception to the rule is when you write a book. Books are written to strict word counts. Too few and the book looks thin and people won't buy it. Too many words means the book looks weighty and, again, people will be put off buying it.

Here are some good ways to lead opinion:

• Add short relevant comments to blogs and news pieces that are likely to be widely read.

• Become an enthusiastic user of Twitter to:

  ° comment on what respected commentators have tweeted, modifying to add your thought (MT) rather than simply retweeting (RT)

  ° reply to tweets if you feel qualified to challenge them and, more importantly, their writer – the debate will get you noticed.

• Stay on the right side of the fine line between being controversial and being potentially libellous.

Finally, here are some very practical things you can do to be seen as an opinion leader:

• Ask questions when others choose to remain silent.

• Stand up for what you feel to be important and be able to explain why.

• Challenge what you see to be unjust or wrong.

• Make time for those who ask your advice.

> WOMEN'S ISSUES HAVE ALWAYS BEEN A PART OF MY LIFE. MY GOAL IS TO BRING THE WORD 'FEMINISM' BACK INTO THE ZEITGEIST AND REFRAME IT.'
>
> ANNIE LENNOX

> ## ! Be an authority
>
> Summarize the opportunities you see using words other people will remember.

In this chapter you've discovered:

- that it is important to embrace what is new and then help others do the same
- that, to become influential, it helps to have the support of influential people
- that it's as much *how* you say it as *what* you say that people remember.

13.
Teamwork – how to influence people you may not manage

Working together

Nobody works in complete isolation. Even the most remote lighthouse keeper relied on colleagues delivering supplies and taking over when time was needed ashore. We all rely on the co-operation of those around us to succeed at work.

In an ideal world, everyone would work together in complete harmony. There would never be any problems. Equipment would never go wrong and people would never go sick. But, of course, we live in a world filled with unpredictable and often unexpected occurrences, which means that we often need people to go that little bit further to help us.

Imagine for a moment that there are two lighthouse keepers. Both spend weeks on end stuck on virtually inaccessible rocky outcrops at opposite ends of a wide bay. One is a fairly laid-back guy who bakes cakes and plays the guitar to while away the long, lonely hours. The other is never happy and spends much of his time complaining about the weather, faulty equipment and, worst of all, members of the support team.

Which keeper do you think gets the most help from his colleagues? Which gets fresh eggs delivered every week in exchange for a large slice of delicious cake? Which played and sang at the boatman's daughter's wedding? Yes, the nice guy gets far more support than the grumpy one. It's human nature to be most helpful to the people we like.

Take a look around your own organization. However large or small, you can probably name the people who people go out of their way to help. You can also probably think of people everyone tries to avoid. It's not always their fault. Some people have been let down badly by others and find it difficult to form positive relationships with colleagues. Even if you work for yourself, there will be people in your 'virtual team' who fit these descriptions. It's the way people are.

The simple fact is that, if you want to get on, you have to get on with other people. More importantly, you need to get others on your side. Getting others to go out of their way to help you succeed is not only about being nice, it's also about being persuasive.

> 'TO BE PERSUASIVE WE MUST BE BELIEVABLE; TO BE BELIEVABLE WE MUST BE CREDIBLE; TO BE CREDIBLE WE MUST BE TRUTHFUL.'
>
> EDWARD R. MURROW, AMERICAN SECOND WORLD WAR BROADCAST JOURNALIST

! Lead without authority

You don't have to manage a team, just lead it.

Know your 'halo'

There's an interesting management term called 'the halo effect'. It refers to the fact that managers can be swayed by one outstanding attribute in a team member to the extent that they overlook glaring deficiencies. For example, a bar owner might hire people because they look attractive and overlook the fact that they are terrible at arithmetic. The result could be that customers spend more, but profits are eroded by the bar staff charging the wrong prices.

Management judgement can be biased by a 'halo' for many reasons. The problem is twofold. On the one hand, the admired attribute or interest can make the halo wearer the boss's favourite. But, on the other hand, that favouritism can cause resentment within the team. That, in turn, makes it harder for the favourite to succeed and, often, colleagues will try to 'show up' their shortcomings, frequently in quite damaging ways.

Now, all this doesn't mean that you should not make sure your boss can see your halo. It means you need to be sensitive to the impact any favouritism might have on those around you. In other words, while, at first glance, being the office star in the boss's eyes might be a goal, in reality it is just one part of your strategy to get on.

It's good to have a competitive advantage over colleagues and often better to have the ear of the boss. But to keep your colleagues on your side you need to use your position to their benefit as well as your own.

> **! Lead without authority**
>
> Don't just polish your halo; use it to reflect light on those who work alongside you.

Groundwork

As with all aspects of sales, preparation is everything. It's no good waiting until you want the whole team to work late on your project to win them over. You need to get them on your side now and keep them there, ready for when you need to call in favours.

Look on it as a 'bank of favours'. The more you deposit as favours done for others, the easier it will be to make an urgent withdrawal when you need stuff done. Actually, it's more complicated than just bestowing favours and doing good deeds. Just as you have to work hard at becoming the authoritative 'go to' person, it takes considerable effort to pull in the kind of help that can make or break your career.

To do the groundwork, you need to influence three things:

1 politics
2 propaganda
3 planted ideas.

Let's explore each of these in turn and see how selling skills can enable you to turn each to your advantage.

Politics

We've all experienced the benefits and drawbacks of office politics. It's what can make simple things surprisingly complicated and difficult things surprisingly simple. Office politics is all about influence and power. Manage the office politics and you become someone who can get things done. Ignore the office politics and you can find yourself facing seemingly insurmountable barriers to success.

All communities are political, and organizations are certainly no exception. There will be groups or factions, each looking after their own interests. There will be people wielding power and influence, without necessarily being committed to the boardroom vision. Lastly, there will be people able to play the politics and succeed, as well as those who choose to challenge rather than play ball. All too often, they are beaten.

Politics is what prompts people who arrive in an organization with fresh ideas to become quickly disillusioned and leave. It's something you need to manage if you are to see your ideas adopted and your opportunities increase.

To manage and exploit the politics in your organization, you need to:

- identify the power base and build rapport with those who really influence what goes on
- clearly demonstrate how your agenda aligns positively with theirs
- allow people to see that, while you will clearly benefit, so too will they
- build and manage an internal network of supporters across your organization
- never forget that some very junior people can have a very big influence over what happens.

Managing office politics so that it helps rather than hinders you requires all the selling skills described in this book. You need to ask the right questions, identify and counter likely objections and gain commitment to tangible action.

> 'I AM EXTRAORDINARILY PATIENT, PROVIDED I GET MY OWN WAY IN THE END.'
>
> MARGARET THATCHER

! Lead without authority

Managing office politics is like playing chess – you need to keep a few moves ahead of an opponent.

Propaganda

In the Second World War my late uncle served in the Fleet Air Arm. One of many assignments he undertook was to throw leaflets out of small planes low over enemy-held territory. These leaflets were written to encourage enemy troops to surrender, by suggesting they faced little hope of victory and a very real chance of imminent, painful death. This is propaganda.

Propaganda is a powerful tool and can undermine and subvert. In an organizational world, starting and spreading rumours can destroy a large corporation, especially if picked up by the media. 'There's no smoke without fire' is the classic response. Doubt is often all that is needed to force a change of direction. It's why social media is so powerful today, and also why it is potentially so dangerous. Good propaganda has to appeal, but it does not necessarily have to be true.

Here are some points to consider if you want to use propaganda to further your cause:

- Only use propaganda to promote your idea, not undermine someone else's. Embarking on anything negative or destructive will backfire and do your career harm.

- Use memorable phrases to summarize your message and make it easier for others to share.

- Make the benefits to others obvious, measurable and relevant to their needs.

- Be wary of involving people outside your organization in your campaign to change things within it.

Finally, here's an example of how propaganda can work. Imagine that you manage the café in a garden centre. You want more space to accommodate more tables but this means a major reshuffle of all the displays. Ideally, some sections would move outside to make room.

You've made the business case to the boss and in principle she agrees. However, she is equally keen not to rock the boat with the other managers and refuses to commit to a date for the reorganization of the sales floor.

To succeed, you need the other managers to lobby on your behalf for what at first glance gives you more space and them less. So you set out to help them see how, by helping you, they are helping themselves.

You work out that colleagues selling higher-value items would benefit if customers had the opportunity to have time to think about their purchase over a coffee. You tell them that this might be useful to them, then do some research to show how this might influence sales across the garden centre.

Your tactics include:

- leaving relevant trade magazine articles in the staff room for colleagues to read
- working out what the additional sales might mean to the other managers in terms of their sales bonuses – say another £250 per annum each
- talking a lot about what £250 can buy, for example a weekend break or tickets for a major sporting event.

Then you raise the issue again at the next team meeting and ask your colleagues whether they'd mind the upheaval that could lead to higher bonuses.

> 'IT'S SO EASY FOR PROPAGANDA TO WORK, AND DISSENT TO BE MOCKED.'
>
> HAROLD PINTER

Planting ideas

Your colleagues will have a far greater sense of ownership of any project if they think elements of it were their own ideas. We all feel more committed to things we had a hand in developing than those thrust upon us by others. This is especially true if the originator of the idea is not your boss.

So, to win support for your project, idea or concept, you have to help other people take ownership of the idea, even before it is fully formed. This means involving people in the development of the idea. Hardest of all, it means letting go of control a little.

In fact, you only become a true leader when you can comfortably celebrate when someone else enjoys well-deserved recognition for taking your idea and making it work. Leaders are people more concerned with getting the job done than who gets the credit.

Perhaps the best way to plant ideas is to organize informal project meetings. In a large organization, these can take place over lunch in the canteen. In a smaller organization, you need either to bring in sandwiches or to go to a local café. What's important is for you to buy the coffee, because, subconsciously, those you invite will feel indebted to you – if only slightly.

Next you have to sell the idea. That means using all of the techniques described in Part 1 of this book. People need to:

• understand what your idea means to them, ideally in tangible terms
• have some soft benefits (recognition and status)
• feel that they have been able to play a part in designing the package
• have the opportunity to share any concerns and have them satisfactorily dealt with
• know that the idea has (or will soon have) the support of the organization.

If you can manage all of these things, you will have done the groundwork and be ready to make things happen.

Leading change

If you have vision, take the initiative and involve colleagues across your organization to make things happen, you will be leading change. This will boost your standing as an authoritative 'go to' person. It will also build your profile and reputation, both within the organization and elsewhere. In short, it will open doors and bring opportunity.

At a very practical level, what are the day-to-day techniques you need to use? As well as the planned activities described already, you may need to adapt your behaviour. By that I do not mean to say that you should dramatically change the way you are, because that would not be sustainable. It's more about becoming just a little more controlled, thoughtful and self-aware.

Here are some things that might help you day to day. Why not try to make habits of some of them:

• **Question** – encourage people to reflect on and explain what they are doing and why. By gently challenging their assumptions you will give them greater focus and clarity of purpose.
• **Empower** – delegate as much as you can and trust people to do their best. Accept that they may do things differently from you, but, equally, that your way is not always going to be the best.

- **Trust** – trust others to get things done without being nagged or reminded. Micro-managing kills trust in those who report to you. It's even more damaging when applied to those you don't directly manage.

- **Agree goals** – agreeing lots of simple short-term goals makes it easy for people to know what you want and, more importantly, to know when it's been done.

- **Be realistic** – it's no good asking for the impossible then shouting when it's not achieved. You have to be realistic and remember that, however persuasive you may be, people have only a finite amount of time and energy.

- **Take the blame** – never delegate blame, but instead take the rap yourself. People will take greater risks for you if they know you will not leave them stranded if it starts to go wrong.

- **Ask for feedback** – and make sure that people know you are willing to listen. Furthermore, be sure to accept negative feedback. It tells you how people are feeling as well as what's not working.

- **Give respect** – not everyone sees the world as you do. You have to respect differences of opinion and recognize that you won't win everyone over. Learn to respect those who oppose you and they in turn will become more respectful of your perspective and ambition.

- **Concede** – it's only when you start a project that the hidden pitfalls begin to reveal themselves. Be prepared to adapt and even change direction. There's nothing wrong with conceding on some aspects of the work if the result is still in line with your vision.

- **Get involved** – lead from the front and get involved. You'll win more support if you are willing to do at least some of the nastier tasks yourself. It's why good sales managers make cold calls.

- **Show humility** – you are trying to change things and, of course, that will benefit your career. But recognize that others should benefit, too, and have the humility to share the praise when it starts to flow. The people who matter most will always recognize your role, even if you're not standing in the limelight.

'DON'T JUDGE EACH DAY BY THE HARVEST YOU REAP BUT BY THE SEEDS THAT YOU PLANT.'

ROBERT LOUIS STEVENSON

! **Lead without authority**

It's more important to be respected than liked, although being liked helps, too.

There's a very fine line between being the popular, 'go to' person in a team who makes things happen and builds a following and being annoying, self-centred and overly demanding of others.

You need to tread the line sensitively, carefully, and with your eyes and ears open. Remember that you will at times get it wrong and create tension. The good news is that people soon forget and there are few situations that cannot be recovered, or at least healed, over time. Never forget that you need the help others can give to succeed.

In this chapter you've discovered:

- that you can achieve more if you have people from across your organization willing to help, even when it's not part of their job to do so

- that highlighting the strengths of others will get you further than simply highlighting your own

- that propaganda can be very effective at encouraging positive change.

14.
Bosses – managing your manager

Management today

Management style has evolved enormously over the past 100 years. Whereas once bosses issued commands and expected unquestioning obedience, the workplace is now far more collaborative.

Perhaps the First World War provides the best example of 'command and control' management. That is where the team is taught how to do the job but it is not considered necessary for them to know why it's important.

Sure, the men in the trenches knew they were there to win a war, but the generals developed the strategy and then issued orders to the front-line officers. When they blew the whistle and the men went over the top, they knew they faced mud and bullets. But few would have been told how their advance contributed to the overall goal. Questioning orders was discouraged and to challenge meant to risk being branded a coward.

In complete contrast, when Ricardo Semler took over his father's white-goods manufacturing business in the 1980s, he created one of the world's most democratic companies. He overturned his father's autocratic, command-and-control structure and broke the company down into semi-autonomous, self-managing units.

This meant that teams knew exactly what they had to do and, moreover, had the authority to follow their instinct and not the rule book. Teams set their own pay and work hours, purchased the materials they needed, and sold on to other teams the products they had created.

So, for example, the team making printed circuit boards knew that, if they charged too much, the team assembling the washing machines would make products too expensive for the marketplace. They also knew the importance of fulfilling orders on time. This meant tighter cost control, flexible working and, above all else, people who felt empowered, enabled and, to a large extent, in control.

By creating an internal, dynamic economy, Semler's company became more resilient and therefore more successful. If your firm is a little traditional in its management style, you can start to change that by using selling techniques to 'manage' your boss.

'THE SPEED OF THE BOSS IS THE SPEED OF THE TEAM.'

LEE IACOCCA

> **! Manage the boss**
>
> More often than not, the more democratically an organization is managed, the more successful it will become.

Knowing your boss

To manage your boss you have to first understand your boss. How long has she or he worked for the organization? Did they start at the bottom and work up, or even found the business? Or did they join recently to bring about change of some kind? Their history, experience, objectives, values and attitudes will all shape their management style. The better you know them, the better you can influence them.

You often find, particularly in small organizations, that bosses hire people like themselves. This is not necessarily the best thing because, of course, the best teams are usually made up of quite different people. But it will often be the case that those who hold the power where you work have similar outlooks.

This shapes the culture of the organization and can make it harder to change things from the shop or office floor. Here are some different management traits and how best to work with them:

• **Driven** – if you report to someone who arrives early, works late and talks about nothing but work, it can be challenging. Often the driven, workaholic boss expects you to make huge sacrifices for work, too, even though there may be less benefit for you in doing so. Manage your driven boss by:

   ° making sure that you have measurable goals and deadlines for your work, and making sure that he knows when you meet them

- putting in the extra time when it's needed, but also being firm and leaving on time when it's not.

- **Reclusive** – this is the boss who has nothing from home in his office, not even a picture of her kids. She comes to work, does everything expected of her, helps you when asked and then goes home bang on time. You've worked for her for five years and still don't know her partner's name. Manage her by:

  - respecting her wish to keep home and work separate and doing the same – she won't want to hear about your holiday, just to know that you're back

  - taking as much responsibility for your work as she will allow, then just getting on with it – she'll ask if she's worried; you'll find over time that you can take more control, a little bit at a time.

- **Political** – in large organizations some people climb the career ladder by reading and managing the politics. This boss is more interested in what's happening internally than in the wider world outside. He probably has a great network and can be a little ruthless, too, if someone gets in his way. Manage him by:

  - keeping him fed with titbits of gossip from your own network

  - selling him the benefits of letting you take things where you feel they should go.

- **Butterfly** – she has a short attention span and forgets everything you've said when you leave the room. But, conversely, she is highly creative and widely respected for the innovation she brings. Manage her by:

  - taking away the detail and bureaucracy and building your own power base as her fixer

  - building your value to her by supporting her new ideas and not being afraid to challenge her constructively if you have doubts.

- **Stressed** – too often, people dump stress on those further down the structure. This boss feels the weight of the whole company's problems on his shoulders and worries incessantly. He can become very picky over detail, if only because that's all he feels within his power to control. Manage him by:

  - becoming a sounding board, winning his confidence and listening when he wants to unburden

  - volunteering to take on the stuff he worries about as this will build your standing and make you indispensable.

Finally, here are three tips that will help you whatever type of boss you have:

1 Have regular meetings to review your work and progress and create an agenda so that nothing important gets left out.

2 Always preface discussion about a project with a quick recap of the goals and timeline.

3 Talk as much about how *they* will benefit as you do about what's in it for you.

'WE ARE MADE WISE NOT BY THE RECOLLECTION OF OUR PAST, BUT BY THE RESPONSIBILITY FOR OUR FUTURE.'

GEORGE BERNARD SHAW

> **! Manage the boss**
>
> The easier you make life for your boss, the easier it becomes to make your own life as easy or hard as you choose.

Wear your boss's shoes

When I was a young sales rep, I had two rather negative beliefs. The first was that, whatever the sales figures might say to the contrary, I was far from being a top performer. The second was that my boss was an idiot.

Then I was invited to cover for my boss for a fortnight while he went on holiday. This meant that, for the first time, I was able to see how the others in my team performed. Some were always behind with their paperwork, others were almost impossible to contact (this was before email and mobile phones), and, worst of all, one had made giving customers discounts the rule rather than the exception.

But, as well as being hugely motivating, it was also rather frustrating. You see, I had to complete my boss's weekly reports to his boss and this was almost impossible. His boss took me to one side and showed me how all the sales data was used for production planning. He explained why it was so important for the sales team to forecast accurately. I realized the perils of making products nobody wanted and then running out of the products everyone did want.

Above all else, that experience gave me an insight into what management was all about. Now able to see my own performance in context and having had a glimpse of the bigger picture, I wanted more and started my ascent on the corporate ladder.

Even if you cannot get the opportunity to deputize for your boss for a week or two, do make the effort to see work through their eyes. Remember that, to sell them the idea of helping you, it is first vital to strengthen your rapport.

'WHEN YOU BECOME A PARENT, YOU LOOK AT YOUR PARENTS DIFFERENTLY. YOU LOOK AT BEING A CHILD DIFFERENTLY. IT'S AN AWAKENING, A REVELATION THAT YOU HAVE.'

PHILIP SEYMOUR HOFFMAN

! Manage the boss

The more clearly you can see the world through your boss's eyes, the easier it will become to direct their attention towards the achievements you want to make.

Taking the lead

You have goals. You also have a boss and need them to endorse and support your endeavours. Clearly, the more closely aligned your ambition is with that of your boss and the organization, the easier it will be to win and maintain her or his support.

There are some techniques that can help you keep your boss's focus on your agenda as well as their own. In most organizations, the overall goal is broken down and delegated to department heads, who then break the goals down further and delegate some more.

The closer you are to the top, the bigger and more strategic your goals. By the time the goals reach the bottom of the corporate mountain, they may simply be a series of 'key performance indicators'. For example, the person who cleans the toilets has to sign a sheet on the washroom wall hourly, to show they've inspected and tidied up. While important, especially for visitors, this bears little relationship to the overall business objective.

So, while taking the lead is easier the further up the ladder you are, it's not impossible at any level. Remember how in Chapter 11 we looked at how to become an authority or 'go to' person. Everyone can create their niche.

Perhaps the most effective way to take the lead is to set an agenda for meetings with your boss. This needs to be structured to include:

- **update** – progress against projects you've been asked to complete
- **right now** – a quick SWOT analysis to highlight strengths, weaknesses, opportunities and threats to your success
- **future** – where you want things to go (presented as features and benefits).

Here is an example:

- The update can cover your performance targets as well as specific short-term projects. Always summarize in terms of percentages, as well as actuals, even if not numeric goals (e.g. 'warehouse reorganization: 50 per cent complete).
- The SWOT is your opportunity both to show you understand the bigger picture and to raise the need for additional resources to overcome looming barriers. Present these as cost and return, or feature and benefit. (e.g. 'If I can spend an extra £200 this week on agency staff, I will be able to complete both orders for Ireland and ship them together. That saves £300 so makes us £100').
- And then, having covered all that is probably on your boss's mind, you can share some of the things on yours. This is where you can talk about your own development needs, courses you have seen and wish to do, or opportunities you wish to take. Again, always quantify in terms of cost and return.

Because you work with your boss all the time, the earlier parts of the sales process (establishing rapport and creating interest) are less important. But don't neglect the correct use of open and closed questions to get information and gain commitment.

Remember that effective questioning will enable you to overcome your boss's objections more easily. You may well be competing for resources and, not least, your boss's time. Show how you can make good use of both and deliver a tangible return on investment, and both you and your boss can win. After all, one of the measures of a boss's performance is the achievements of the team they manage.

LEADERSHIP IS SOLVING PROBLEMS. THE DAY SOLDIERS STOP BRINGING YOU THEIR PROBLEMS IS THE DAY YOU HAVE STOPPED LEADING THEM. THEY HAVE EITHER LOST CONFIDENCE THAT YOU CAN HELP OR CONCLUDED YOU DO NOT CARE. EITHER CASE IS A FAILURE OF LEADERSHIP.

COLIN POWELL

! Manage the boss

Setting the agenda for a meeting is like bowling in cricket. You lob the balls and others will automatically reach out to bat them.

Prioritizing

How often have you made a mobile phone call from a bus or train and lost the connection before getting to the point you really called to discuss? It happens to us all, particularly those of a naturally chatty disposition. Of course, it's important to open a conversation with some small talk, but it's more important to get to the point. In any selling situation, there's always the risk of distraction spoiling the moment and stealing your opportunity.

So, as well as setting an agenda for meetings, you need to prioritize the things you want to discuss whenever you meet your boss. Clearly, top of the list will be the things the boss considers most important. But your priorities are important, too.

When you have a long list of things to cover, try pruning it down to the three most important. The reason for this can be explained using the 'Rule of Three', which says that we all find it easier to receive information in groups of three. This is true in writing, presenting and even telling jokes – and illustrated by this last sentence!

It is no coincidence that there were three wise men in the Christian Christmas story, or that Goldilocks encountered three bears. The Rule of Three has always been applied to storytelling and works in pretty much any situation.

We'll talk more about this in the next chapter, which covers making presentations. But the point to take from this section is this: if you go to your boss with a list of four or five points to discuss, there's a very real chance that only the first three will receive serious attention.

Problems and solutions

Selling is all about identifying problems and providing solutions to them. Yet, too often, we simply present our bosses with problems, and leave it to them to find the solution. I'm sure that you know and perhaps work with people who delight in reporting a problem yet never suggest a solution. They'll say, 'That's the boss's job not mine.'

But you are ambitious and want to get on. Furthermore, sometimes you'll be able to suggest a solution that's to your advantage. This might be immediate or of greater long-term strategic value to your career.

For example, someone needs to urgently deliver and replace a broken component at a customer's premises in New York. You report the problem and then volunteer to go yourself. You get to enjoy a free weekend in a city you've long wanted to visit.

Even if your boss is quite autocratic and controlling, you can do the legwork for them and suggest solutions. If they're more laid back, you can simply solve the problem yourself and simply tell them about both the issue and the solution. This shows your willingness to take responsibility.

If, on the other hand, you have no idea how to solve the problem, why not ask colleagues for suggestions before admitting to your boss that you don't know the answer?

The worst thing you can do is to simply pass on the problem to your boss with no comment at all. Customer complaint emails that are just forwarded to the boss with no comment are one of the most annoying things a boss can receive. Always present solutions as well as problems.

'THE PRICE OF GREATNESS IS RESPONSIBILITY.'

WINSTON CHURCHILL

! Manage the boss

The easier you make life for your boss, the easier life can become for you.

In this chapter you've discovered:

- that organizations that delegate authority do better than those that control
- the importance of understanding and working with your boss's management style
- that presenting solutions as well as problems can get you a long way.

15.

Presentations – how to make a powerful pitch

Public speaking

Nobody walks to the front of the room to make a presentation without feeling nervous. You become very aware that everyone's attention has turned to you. However carefully you have prepared, you worry about your content, your slides (if you have them) and, of course, the technology. There is so much that can go wrong and you desperately want it to go well.

Adrenaline is a vital component of every successful presentation. It's the hormone we produce when we feel threatened. The mounting anxiety we all feel in those final minutes before we take the floor prompts our bodies to release adrenaline. This:

• increases our heart rate and makes us stronger
• gives the rush of energy needed to perform at our very best
• heightens our senses and makes us more aware of how our audience is reacting.

Then, when you've finished and sat down, you feel a tremendous feeling of anticlimax. You slump, physically and mentally. That's normal, too, because the danger has passed and your body needs to recover and return to normal.

I do a lot of public speaking, sometimes in front of large conference audiences. In common with most professional speakers, I have a warm-up ritual I try to follow as I limber up for my performance. Mine involves extra-strong coffee, chocolate cake and, inevitably, a visit to the toilet. The cake energizes, the coffee stimulates and the toilet visit provides time for some final moments of quiet contemplation.

If you are going to become successful at selling, even if only within your organization, you need to be able to present confidently. Once you recognize that, even if they don't show it, everyone is a little nervous when they present to a group, you will automatically become a more confident presenter yourself.

Humour

Used effectively, humour relaxes an audience and makes your messages more memorable. That's not to suggest that you turn your talk into a stand-up routine. You need to be very polished and professional to tell jokes to an audience successfully. Instead, just look for and share the funny side of your subject.

All good presentations involve storytelling and the best stories are those that contain humour. Think back to the things that have happened to you over the years. I expect that there are lots of very relevant amusing anecdotes you can build into your presentations.

Providing you don't knock yourself too hard, self-deprecating humour can be very powerful, too. It's often best used as a way of establishing rapport with your audience at the start. For example, I might start by telling a conference audience about my chocolate cake and coffee routine, explaining that, unless they smile, I might need a second slice right now. Remember that telling your audience you are nervous is fine, providing you do it in the right way – that is, without being too negative.

Humour can also be a great way to defuse the tension that can follow when you are asked a very difficult question. Replying in a way that makes the audience smile will keep them on your side.

Here are some tips to help you use humour when presenting:

- **About you** – the best presentation humour involves telling stories about things that have happened to you. This also avoids the risk of making jokes at the expense of others, which can backfire and cause offence.
- **Timing is everything** – leaving a pause between story and punch line will build both suspense and impact.

- **A picture** – it's so true that a picture can save a thousand words. A well-chosen slide can give a humorous slant to something everyone in the room is familiar with.
- **Ration humour** – it's good to start and end with a laugh; you can also use humour to emphasize a key point.

During a typical presentation you will need to make some serious, even sombre points. Humour allows you to lift the audience up again after they've contemplated the bad news you may have to deliver. With practice, you'll find you can influence the mood of your audience to a large extent. You can take them down to contemplate some unpleasant issue, then lift them quickly again using humour.

'I DO A LOT OF PUBLIC SPEAKING AND PRESENTATIONS AND I'LL ALWAYS START WITH A SELF-DEPRECATING JOKE TO MAKE EVERYBODY FEEL COMFORTABLE WITH MY SIZE BECAUSE THERE CAN BE HANG-UPS AND ANXIETIES.'

WARWICK DAVIES (ENGLISH ACTOR WITH DWARFISM)

> **!** **Present well**
>
> Humour makes it easier for your audience to laugh with you than at you.

Storytelling

There's nothing quite as compelling as a good story. Storytelling is how we learned before writing was invented. A story brings a message to life in a way nothing else can; it connects with us in a deep and emotional way. It's how religions spread their messages and why we sometimes cry in movies.

If you tell stories when presenting, you will connect more deeply with your audience. That's equally true when you are presenting to one person as when you are addressing one thousand. It's all about painting pictures in the mind of each audience member. Most of all, it's about helping them imagine themselves experiencing the situation you are describing.

Examples of storytelling in the workplace include:

- **Success stories** – telling how others have benefitted from, say, an expensive training course will make your boss far more likely to pay for you to attend.

- **Parables** – verbal analogies you make up to illustrate your point in a non-controversial way can be useful when you want to confront your audience with something about which they may be sensitive.

- **Visual prompts** – this is where you place an object on the table and then use it to illustrate your point (e.g. you use a broken car headlight as a prompt to tell a story about poor driving).

You don't need to tell long or complicated stories. In fact, some of the most memorable will be the shortest. To be most effective, your story needs to describe a journey through adversity to success. To do this it needs to contain:

- **a hero** – the person who overcomes ...
- **a problem** – that's between the hero and ...
- **the reward** – the reason the problem was tackled.

Additionally, as well as the story you are telling, there has to be an underlying 'real story', which is the point you are setting out to make.

Nursery rhymes are great examples of good storytelling. For example:

> *Doctor Foster went to Gloucester,*
> *In a shower of rain;*
> *He stepped in a puddle,*
> *Right up to his middle,*
> *And never went there again.*

Mothers told the Doctor Foster story to their children to warn them that puddles in the road can be much deeper than they look. The story is said to date back to the thirteenth century when roads were rough tracks and often contained very deep puddles.

Note how the story rhymes. This gives rhythm and makes it easier to remember.

Lastly, as you think about how to use storytelling in your next presentation, here are some tips:

- Give your stories context and explain how you came to see or hear them.
- Move about, perhaps turning when describing dialogue to represent each speaker.
- Use your hands to emphasize key points.
- Speak slowly and pause after describing the problem or challenge in order to create suspense.
- Ask your audience questions and pull them into the story.

Perhaps the greatest benefit of storytelling is that your audience will remember the stories you tell more than any other part of your presentation. What's more, they are likely to share them with others. Telling stories is a great way to spread the word.

'STORYTELLING IS ABOUT TWO THINGS; IT'S ABOUT CHARACTER AND PLOT.'

GEORGE LUCAS

Positive and negative

It has to be said that, for the majority of people, the glass is more often half empty than half full. That's in part because we tend to take the good things for granted and take more notice of things we feel are holding us back. The fact is, it is very easy to focus on the negatives, and it's an attitude that, when you are presenting, can significantly reduce your effectiveness.

To counter this, you need to make a conscious effort to make positive, not negative, points when you present. Of course, you have to explain the downside of not accepting your recommendation, but you need to put a greater emphasis on the positives. Storytelling can give you a framework within which to place the negatives. For example: 'We're good guys, this nasty thing is all that stands between us and success, so by doing this, this and this we can be celebrating our success within a week.'

Reflect on recent presentations you have made and indeed on your worldview in general. Make a list of the opportunities and threats facing you right now. Then add them up and see which list is longer! Ideally, you'll see twice as many opportunities as threats.

When preparing a presentation, it will help you to consider these five points:

1 However bad your luck has been recently, accept that the world is not against you.

2 You cannot change the past, and people will forget your bad stuff faster if you don't dwell on it.

3 Be realistic and honest about the downside but make sure the upside you describe is bigger.

4 Remember that not everyone will agree with and welcome the debate this prompts.

5 Recognize that the future is largely what you choose to make it.

> POSITIVE THINKING WILL LET YOU DO EVERYTHING BETTER THAN NEGATIVE THINKING WILL.
>
> ZIG ZIGLAR

Structure

Good presentations are logically structured and easy to follow. This means clear signposting and letting your audience know as you move from stage to stage. If you use slides, it's relatively easy to lay out the structure on an early slide and then return to the same slide at each point of transition.

If you want your presentation to sell for you, it has to follow the stages of a sales interview. But, because in this situation you are doing most of the talking, you need also to ask questions on behalf of your audience. These are called 'rhetorical questions' (you ask questions to make a point, not to seek audience feedback).

Your presentation therefore needs to contain the following elements:

- an introduction (attention)
- key messages (interest)
- reasons to act (desire)
- commitment/questions (action)
- a close.

Additionally, you need to apply the Rule of Three wherever possible. This makes the presentation appear more logical and certainly easier to follow.

So summarize your message under three headings, present three reasons to act, and perhaps even offer three alternative solutions for your audience to choose between (one of which should be very easy to do).

Let's cover each section in turn.

Introduction

Your introduction needs to explain:

1 who you are and why you are qualified to speak
2 what you are going to cover in the presentation
3 why this is relevant to your audience.

It also helps to include in your introduction something that grabs attention and stimulates interest. This might be a stark statistic relevant to the subject, or just a humorous take on the subject if there's a risk of it all becoming very dry and boring.

For example:

> *Good morning, my name is Robert Ashton, author of* Sales for Non-Salespeople.
>
> *I'm going to explain to you today why everyone needs to have selling skills and, what's more, I'm going to show you:*
>
> * *that selling is about helping people make decisions, not pushing them*
> * *how being able to sell means being able to get on at home, work and life in general*
> * *why every single person in this room can benefit from learning how to sell.*
>
> *Now let me start with a story ...*

Key messages

As you can see, I have already described my three key messages. I have also told a story (perhaps to illustrate an unusual situation where selling skills came in handy). In this section of the talk, you have to spell out your case. Remember, you are raising awareness of the need. In my case, it's the need for everyone to have selling skills.

Your key messages each need to be spelled out in enough detail to make your audience understand why it's important to them. If you give them too much detail, they will quickly lose interest. And don't worry about not giving them enough information; they will soon ask whether there's anything they don't fully understand.

It can be helpful to deal with each key message in three steps:

1 describe the message

2 illustrate with a story

3 relate the message to the audience.

The final point is the most important of all. It is in effect what salespeople call a 'trial close'. That means asking for commitment in a way that encourages them to tell you what they still need to know to be convinced. In a presentation, it prompts questions. Answering an audience's questions takes you closer to gaining commitment at the end.

Reasons to act

Having made your case, you need to stimulate desire. From Chapter 4 you will remember the importance of creating a sense of urgency. Your reasons need to be both quantified (measurable) and urgent (now or never). Because you have given three key messages, you can now translate each of these into a reason to act.

Imagine for a moment that you are pitching a business idea to the Board of your company. You've already won over your boss, who sits on the Board, but you're competing for budget with three other projects. Hopefully, you have done some research and know the strengths and weaknesses of the competing proposals. The reasons to act section of your presentation needs to:

• summarize the key benefits and quantify them in terms your audience will value most

• without saying as much, show how these benefits outweigh those offered by rival projects

• explain why action/investment is needed now and why it is urgent.

For example, if I was speaking at a conference about selling, I might have as one of my goals to sell signed copies of this book. Someone has kindly come along from a local bookshop with a stock of copies. By offering to sign and dedicate copies bought on the day, I create a sense of urgency. That's because I can only sign and dedicate copies of my book when I am there, not once I've returned home.

Commitment

Now you've got people thinking and answered a few questions, you want to move towards closing the deal. In this section, you summarize the key points very briefly and ask for questions. You might, particularly if you're not convinced you've won total support yet, use rhetorical questions to emphasize any points you feel you need to make. (Perhaps you've thought of a better answer to a question asked earlier.)

For example:

> One question I was asked a lot when researching this proposal was this: how will the gardeners know when to plant the seeds if they're not familiar with the vegetable. My answer was to explain how we'll be printing sowing instructions on the packet and colour-coding the whole range by season to encourage people to keep all their summer seeds together.

If you've played the office politics really well, you might know that this point confronts head on the concern raised by one of the Board when discussing the shortlisted projects over lunch in the canteen.

Close

If you're presenting a proposal to a group, you will need to hand over control to the person chairing the meeting at this point. Perhaps you've been invited to present to a Council about a sports club you want to set up. The vote will need to be asked for by the chairperson of the meeting, not you as someone invited to present.

As well as thanking the audience for their attention and questions, it's good to end with some impact. Ideally, this will link back to your opening. It could be visual if you are using slides, or an epilogue to the story you told in your introduction – perhaps what happened after the event you described at the beginning.

Do invest time and effort in getting your opening and closing just right. A good opening relaxes the audience and boosts your confidence. A good closing gives people a positive memory of your presentation. It also lets them know it's time to give you a round of applause.

'APPLAUSE IS A RECEIPT, NOT A BILL.'

DALE CARNEGIE

> **!** **Present well**
>
> The better you signpost your presentation, the easier it will be for your audience to complete the journey you are laying out for them.

Slides

The most inspirational speakers don't use slides. Instead, they tell stories that paint vivid, lasting pictures in your mind. I once heard Desmond Tutu speak at a conference. The audience stood and clapped as he walked on to the stage. He spoke quietly and slowly and talked about poverty and what we could all do to help alleviate it. Anything on a slide would have detracted from his powerful presence and the important message he had come to convey.

However, like you, I am unlikely to be greeted on any stage by a standing ovation. Unless people already know very clearly who you are and what you stand for, you will probably want to use some slides to illustrate your presentation.

The technology exists to embed video clips, music and even live links that enable your presentation to involve interaction with people on the other side of the planet. That same technology can, if it fails to work properly or you become too preoccupied with it, destroy your presentation.

Here are three golden rules to follow when you use technology:

1 **Less is more** – keep it simple, visual and relevant to your talk.

2 **Must add value** – your slides have to bring something extra; if they don't, don't use them.

3 **Never assume** – however much a technician tells you it's going to work fine, be there early enough to check for yourself.

It also goes without saying that your slides should be much more than simply your notes.

If you do use slides, make sure that they illustrate your points rather than make them on your behalf. Make sure that you have a remote device to move your presentation on, rather than having to bend over to use a laptop. Most importantly of all, make sure that there is a screen (often the laptop driving the presentation) where you can clearly see it without turning round to look over your shoulder. Your eyes should be on the audience, not the screen you're standing in front of.

When preparing slides, remember to make them:

- **legible** – in a large, clear font with good contrast between text and background
- **branded** – perhaps with a strapline that summarizes the action you want the presentation to prompt
- **simple** – just a few words and a picture, graph or chart
- **thought-provoking** – adding an extra dimension to your talk
- **accurate** – when audiences see spelling mistakes, the presentation loses its value
- **change predictably** – avoid those 'clever' but distracting slide transition features.

If you deliver a lot of presentations, it might be helpful to have a design professional create a template presentation you can adapt for each talk. This can boost your personal brand awareness and make your presentation stand out from others.

'AN EXPERT IS SOMEBODY WHO IS MORE THAN 50 MILES FROM HOME, HAS NO RESPONSIBILITY FOR IMPLEMENTING THE ADVICE HE GIVES, AND SHOWS SLIDES.'

EDWIN MEESE (US POLITICIAN)

! Present well

Sometimes, a good presentation of a bad idea can be more successful than a bad presentation of a great idea.

In this chapter you've discovered:

- that everyone gets nervous when asked to make a presentation
- that humour, structure and storytelling are important ingredients in any presentation
- that you should use slides only if they'll be saying something you cannot.

PART IV

Selling to customers

16.
Prospecting – searching for and approaching new customers

Creating campaigns

Imagine that it's your first day in a new job. You've been taken on as the first sales rep ever employed by a growing small business. There are some existing customers to service, but your brief is to double sales within 12 months. This week, you'll be visiting existing customers to introduce yourself. But then what? You're not sure. The products you sell could be used by anyone. You don't know where to start.

In fact, you should start with your sales target. How many units do you need to sell to hit your target? How many will each customer buy? Will these be one-off purchases, such as a PC, or will there be repeat purchases, such as paper for a printer? You need to ask yourself all of these questions and more. Then you can plan a campaign.

Sales campaigns are a great discipline because they are:

• **short term** – over a week or month

• **measurable** – you can quickly see how well you are doing

• **scalable** – you learn what works best, refine the process and do it again.

Most importantly of all, a sales campaign breaks down what might appear an impossible task – for example, to double sales in a year – into a series of programmes of activity that you can immediately see are achievable. Once you have mapped out your campaigns, you can plan the first one in detail and then prospect for new customers.

Good sales campaigns give you the opportunity to focus on:

• **a specific group of prospective customers** – for example, a city or business sector

• **seasonal demand** – say, ice cream in the summer and hot chocolate in the winter

• **recent change** – in the way that the smoking ban in bars created a market for pergolas.

However big, small or varied your sales role, it always makes sense to break it down into campaigns. Not only does this make you more focused and effective, it also makes it easier for those around you to contribute to the sales success. For example, if the stationery firm delivery drivers know you are having a push on colour printers, they can mention this on their rounds.

'IF THINGS ARE GOING UNTOWARDLY ONE MONTH, THEY ARE SURE TO MEND THE NEXT.'

JANE AUSTEN

> **! Sales rule**
>
> Always break your time and targets down into manageable, measurable campaigns.

Setting targets

Selling is all about targets. It's how companies manage their salespeople to deliver the orders they need to cover costs and make a profit. For any organization, it's vital to maintain sales at a level that covers the margins on the products or services sold but also covers the overhead costs and rewards the company shareholders.

For example:

Annual sales	£600,000	£800,000	£1,000,000
Cost of producing goods sold (50 per cent of sales)	£300,000	£400,000	£500,000
Overhead costs (rent, wages etc.)	£300,000	£300,000	£300,000
Profit	£0	£100,000	£200,000

Can you see how increasing sales from £800,000 to £1 million doubles profit? Equally, if sales fall below £600,000, the company cannot cover its overhead costs and becomes unprofitable.

Sales targets can also be used to:

• encourage the sale of the most profitable products

• align customer expectation with production and delivery dates

- clear remaining stocks of 'end-of-line' products that might otherwise be overlooked
- link salespeople's income to their targets using incentive schemes or commission payments.

Here's an example:

> Millie's job is to sell dry dog food. Her company is a small manufacturer and wants to double sales in a year. The food is sold to pet shops and kennels and breeders, in packs that typically feed one dog for one week. So, over a year, a dog will consume 50 packs. Your sales target for the next 12 months is 600,000 packs. Or, to put it another way, the owners of 12,000 dogs have to use your product throughout the year.

So now you have to do some maths:

- Current sales are 300,000 packs a year, but experience says people stay with the company for three years, so to confidently hit 600,000 packs a year you must sell 100,000 to replace lost customers as well as 300,000 more. You now have two clear targets:
  - ° to keep existing customers buying at least 200,000 packs
  - ° to find new customers with the potential to buy 400,000 packs between them.
- On average, customers buy 5,000 packs a year, so you have 40 existing customers. It's fair to assume that these are representative of kennel owners and pet shops, so you can quickly calculate that to sell 400,000 packs to new customers you're also going to need to find 80 new customers.

Next you have to work out how many prospects you need to create those two new customers each week. This is called a backward plan. It works like this:

- Your goal is two new sales per week.
- One in three of the prospects you visit turns into a long-term customer – so you need $2 \times 3 = 6$ new meetings a week.
- You find you have to phone five kennels or pet shops to make an appointment that is kept. That means that, to create those six meetings, you need to make $6 \times 5 = 30$ calls.
- Finally, only half of the people you ring are around to take your call. So for those 30 phone conversations you need to make 60 calls.

Now you know that to obtain two new customers a week you need to make 60 phone calls. Furthermore, by monitoring each ratio you can see what works best and whether any prospect group, say pedigree breeders, deliver better results than others.

Next, you have to find those prospects.

> **! Sales rule**
>
> Monitoring your sales ratios enables you to identify the richest seam in your sales mine and concentrate your digging there.

Defining prospects

As you have learned, you need to find a lot more prospects than you need customers. That's because not all will become customers. Think of your backward plan (above) as a funnel. You need to keep pouring new prospects in at the top to create the right number of new customers dropping out of the bottom.

A good prospect will:

- **have much in common with your existing customers** – in fact, the more they have in common, the more likely they are to buy. Take a look at the customers in a specialist shop or on a group holiday and you will see just how similar people can be.

- **be able to make use of what you are selling** – which sounds obvious, but it may not be. It's very easy to assume, for example, that everyone can drive or uses a mobile phone. Always check or qualify your prospect before spending too much time on them.

- **have the ability and authority to make the purchase** – this is crucially important in a business-to-business context, where the person you meet may need to sell the idea of purchase to a more senior colleague (who, of course, is the person you should be selling to!). When selling significant household purchases, you usually need both partners present to get a sale.

- **be able to pay** – you'd be surprised how many people, particularly small business owners, buy things they need but cannot really afford.
- **have realistic expectations** – some people are impossible to please and do not make good customers.

With experience, you will develop a sixth sense when selling. This will alert you to people who may turn out to be really difficult customers who delay payment or complain without good reason. Often, they are the people you have to try really hard to persuade to buy.

> **! Sales rule**
>
> If it's really hard work to persuade someone to buy, it might be even harder work dealing with them once they become customers.

It often helps to define your perfect customer in terms of what they do, where they go and how they spend their time. This helps you with your search for new customers. For example, a tree surgeon might define his perfect customer as 50, living in a leafy suburb and more likely to read *The Daily Telegraph* than the *Guardian* (or the *The Washington Times* than *The New York Times*). Why? Well, because:

- older people are less likely to tackle big DIY jobs themselves and are better able to afford outside help
- suburban dwellers are less likely than country dwellers to own and use a chainsaw
- *Daily Telegraph* readers tend to have more disposable income than *Guardian* readers.

Once you have defined your target audience, you can go out and look for them.

'THE PURPOSE OF A BUSINESS IS TO CREATE A CUSTOMER.'

PETER DRUCKER

Referred prospects

The most obvious, but too often overlooked, source of prospects is your existing customer base. People tend to mix with people like themselves and so will almost certainly know others with the potential to buy from you. Asking your existing customers for introductions should always be your starting point. These introductions are called 'referrals'.

Many salespeople are reluctant to ask for referrals. They feel that somehow they will undermine the integrity of the customer relationship by asking them for introductions. In fact, most satisfied customers like to be asked for referrals. It shows that you value them for more than just their ability to purchase.

When is the best time to ask for a recommendation? You should initially ask at the time the first decision to buy is made. That is the moment when the new customer is most aware of the features and benefits of your offer. There is also usually a feeling of relief when, after perhaps much questioning and consideration, the decision to buy is finally made.

As soon as you have confirmed the details of the new sale, you should ask for a referral. Say something like: 'Now that you can see how this product/service can benefit you, are there people you know who might also appreciate finding out about the product/service?'

Other ways to generate referrals include:

- giving your customer some leaflets to distribute to their friends
- adding a message to your email signature so that every time you email a customer they are reminded that you are looking for referrals
- offering a modest incentive for introductions that lead to a sale
- placing a sign outside your customers' premises, for example saying 'Windows fitted by xyz' and including your phone number

- asking customers for written or video testimonials that you can then add to your website
- sending out regular customer newsletters, which can both ask for referrals and, most importantly, make sure your that customers stay up to date with everything you can do for them.

! Sales rule

When a customer agrees to give you a referral, ask whether they'd ring them right now and make an appointment for you. If they make the call, you're almost certain to get an appointment.

Cold prospects

Long-established salespeople with a large bank of satisfied customers can get all the new enquiries they need from referrals and reputation. (Chapter 12 covers how to build your reputation by becoming an authority.) The rest of us have to keep topping up our sales pipeline with new, cold prospects.

New prospects can be found by:

- cold-calling, either on the phone or door to door
- marketing and promotion to raise awareness and generate enquiries
- researching online and making individual approaches.

In 1990 I was working for a company hit by an economic recession. They made me redundant and to pay the bills I joined a direct-selling financial services company. That industry was less well regulated then and cold-calling was the recognized way of generating sales enquiries.

On the last day of the one-week induction training course, I was one of a group placed in a small call centre. We each had a telephone, our diary and the phone directory for our local area. We'd also learned some sales scripts and this was the moment of truth. Had we got what it took to succeed, or would we fail?

I opened the directory and found the first person named Smith. My logic was that most cold-callers would start at A and work through, so starting at S gave me a head start. I made 30 cold calls and made two appointments. One of those people kept the appointment and made a purchase.

Later I became more sophisticated. I realized that:

- people with three initials were usually wealthier than those with just one or two first names
- some postcodes yielded better prospects than others
- cold-calling people from the industry I had just left meant we had something in common and that improved my hit rate.

But, although I found I was very good at cold-calling and selling financial services, I did not enjoy it. After ten months I started my own marketing business and have worked for myself ever since.

Let's look at how you can generate new prospects in more detail.

Cold-calling

However much we like to think otherwise, cold-calling still works. It's why you keep answering calls from companies offering you 'no win no fee' help in making compensation claims or selling you investment products. UK regulation to restrict cold calls means many cold phone calls are now made from outside the UK. Random cold-calling is a numbers game: the more calls you make, the more sales you generate. (Increasingly, these calls are made by a computer, typically offering you the option to press 5 to find out more or 9 to opt out.)

The less random you can make your cold calls, the more successful you will be. For example, your firm has just replaced the roof on a house and you knock on every door along the street and say: 'You've probably noticed we're working on the roof at number 25. As your house is a similar age, and it's cheaper for us to keep our scaffolding here than come back later, would you like me to carry out a quick survey to check the condition of your roof?'

If you want to make UK telephone cold calls, you should check first that the numbers you wish to call are not listed with the Telephone Preference Service. This is most easily done by purchasing what is called a 'cleaned list', which is a database from which people who have opted not to receive unsolicited calls have been removed.

When buying a list from a list broker, you can select the search criteria used to build your list. This enables you to narrow down the list to cover only those most likely to match your target customer profile. This also gives you the opportunity to tailor the words you use when making the call. For example: 'Good afternoon; is that Mr Smith? I'm told that you have children at private school. Have you considered insurance that would pay the fees if you were unfortunate enough to lose your job?'

Let's look at the script in detail:

By asking 'Is that Mr Smith' (a closed question) you commit the prospect to open dialogue with you. He can say 'yes' or 'no', or hang up. But because he is not sure who you are yet, he answers.

Next, you say 'I'm told that', which implies that someone known to Mr Smith has recommended you to call. He won't realize that you simply bought a list of parents paying for private education. He will soon tell you whether this is incorrect.

Now you have to make your pitch and say why you're calling. Only if this prompts interest can you move into asking open questions to find out more.

When cold-calling, you use a lot of closed questions and make assumptions that you are on the right track. This can feel a little pushy, so you use gently leading questions and longer sentences to make it less interrogative.

! Sales rule

Don't rush to fill the silence when making cold calls. You've caught your prospect off guard by making the call. The longer they stay on the line, the greater your chances of success.

Marketing and promotion

This is not a book about marketing. However, professional marketing and publicity campaigns can be very effective ways to generate sales enquiries. Anyone who responds to a marketing campaign is expressing interest in the offer. They've probably thought a little about how it might benefit them and decided that they can probably afford to purchase.

If you have the chance to influence marketing campaigns in your organization, encourage the team to think beyond the obvious. I once advised a will-writing company to place word-search competitions in their local free newspaper. The hidden words all related to inheritance and there was a prize draw each week to encourage people to send their completed grids in. The campaign ran for many years and was a huge success because:

- people who use a will writer rather than a solicitor are more likely to complete a word search than, say, a crossword puzzle
- searching for words such as 'inheritance tax' and 'intestate' highlighted the very concerns my client was able to solve
- everyone who sent in their competition entry was offered a 'special offer' if they had my client write their will within the next three months.

Effective ways to generate enquiries include:
- advertising with an incentive to respond for more information
- competitions
- sponsorship (e.g. 'For every quotation we issue we'll donate £5 to the local hospice')
- testimonial advertising or celebrity endorsement

In general, marketing and promotion deliver better sales leads than cold-calling. And cold-calling works better, too, if timed to coincide with a marketing campaign to raise awareness.

! Sales rule

The only people who respond to marketing campaigns with no intention of ever buying from you are competitors checking out your offer.

Research and approach

The wealth of data at your fingertips online makes it easier than ever to identify prospective new customers. Where previous generations of salespeople depended on printed directories and newspaper reports to identify the best people to approach, now it's far easier online.

Once you have a clear picture of the characteristics your best customers share, you can then search quite easily for similar people. Here are some tips to help you search more successfully online:

- **quotation marks** – these limit your search to the "exact phrase" rather than the two words separately
- **&** – this will show only those sites where both search terms are listed (e.g. "fried eggs" & bacon)
- **numbers** – remember you can search for number sequences as well as words. So, if you want to find hotels in the Norwich area of England, you can search for hotels & 01603 (which is the area telephone code).

And when searching online, remember:

- **LinkedIn** – search contacts of customers and ask to be introduced
- **client lists** – some professional practices list clients on their websites
- **exhibitor lists** – check out trade show websites – often they give contact names and sometimes even mobile phone numbers
- **memberships lists** – Chambers of Commerce, clubs, associations and more.

Finally, if you know the search criteria that deliver the best results, set up a Google Alert. This means you get an email with links to all new references to your search criteria. (Set one up to let you know whenever you or your firm is mentioned online.)

Having identified your prospects online, you need to approach them. The more personal you can make the approach, the more likely they are to respond. You can send an email or post a letter. Both have their advantages.

Letter	Email
Has more impact	Is faster and cheaper to send
Can enclose literature	Can include hyperlinks to relevant web references
Usually needs a follow-up phone call	Easy for prospect to click reply and enquire
Often best when selling to householders	Often best when selling to businesses

When making a written approach:

- keep it short and to the point – a maximum of 200 words for a letter and 150 words for an email
- use simple language and be explicit – write it as you'd say it and avoid clichés
- make it personal – let the prospect know they're not just being spammed
- ask questions then answer them – this has more impact
- make it easy to respond – use a prepaid reply envelope or suggest phone call or email
- follow up within three days if possible.

Here is a sample cold-approach email:

Dear Chris,

I noticed that you are planning a charity sky dive later this year. Congratulations on your courage!

Knowing how hard it can be to win sponsorship, I thought you might be interested in the recently published book *Sales for Non-Salespeople*.

You might ask me why this book can help. I'd say because, by applying the simple sales techniques it contains, you can help yourself to become just that little bit more persuasive. Ask yourself this: how many sponsors do you need to win to make this £13.99 price of the book a very sound investment?

You can click here and buy a copy on Amazon, or click reply and order a copy signed by the author. I'll give you a ring later in the week to see which you would prefer.

Kind regards,

Andy Sales

Note how the email closes with the promise of a follow-up. This creates a sense of urgency. The recipient has to say 'yes' or 'no', because to say nothing means you're going to ring them. This might sound pushy, but only if it's written in a pushy way.

! Sales rule

When contacting prospective new customers, be proactive rather than relying on your prospect to get in touch if interested. If you want the sale, you need to make the call.

In this chapter you've discovered:

- the value of campaigns in focusing both you and your customers
- that, without clear activity targets, you will find it difficult to hit sales targets
- that the more you know about someone before you approach them, the more likely they are to buy from you.

17.
Customers – how to delight and excite them

Is the customer king?

Many will say that, in any business, the customer is king. In many respects, this is true, because without customers you have no business. Furthermore, if you look back to the activity plan in the last chapter, you will see the importance of maintaining sales volume. In other words, only when you have sold enough to cover your overheads, as well as production costs, do you actually make any money.

However, traditionally, salespeople took the 'customer is king' to also mean that the customer was always right. This clearly can never always be the case. Sometimes, people expect the impossible of you, your firm and your products and services. To accept orders when you are not totally confident yourself that the customer's needs will be met is never a good idea. The disappointed customer will complain not only to you but to anyone else who cares to listen.

If you have done your groundwork, you will have a pretty good idea of what the customer needs. This might not be exactly the same as what they say they want. This is because you will have more experience of what you are selling.

Imagine, for example, that you are selling flooring to householders. You will know from experience that a more expensive, durable vinyl is a wise investment for the kitchen floor of a family with young children. Yet the couple might be on a tight budget and be asking to buy a cheaper product that you know will not last.

Of course, you could simply say 'yes' and take their order. But you owe it to them and yourself to make sure that they fully understand that spending another 20 per cent, say, will give them a floor that will still look good years later. They can then decide, knowing all the facts, which to go for.

Selling successfully is about much more than persuading people to say 'yes'. It is about helping people make the right decision for them, with all the information they need in front of them. Done well, selling creates more than just customers. It creates champions who will recommend you wherever they go.

> 'THERE IS NO HUMAN PROBLEM WHICH COULD NOT BE SOLVED IF PEOPLE WOULD SIMPLY DO AS I ADVISE.'
>
> GORE VIDAL

! Good selling

Successful selling is about meeting needs, not just satisfying wants.

Empathy

To sell effectively, you need to have empathy with your customer. That doesn't mean that you have to like them, but you do need to understand them. What's more, empathy is defined as 'the ability to understand and share the feelings of others'.

If you are enthusiastic about what you sell, you probably already do have some empathy with your customers. It's unlikely that you would sell cars if you were not something of a petrol-head, or clothes if you were not interested in fashion. Remember that your enthusiasm for your product or service will reassure your customer. If it bores you, it will bore your customer, too.

The common interests you have with your customers will help them relate to and trust you. Remember that, to do your job properly, the customer has to believe that your advice is sound. Here are some ways to boost your empathy with your customers:

- **Become a customer** – mystery-shop your competitors and see what it feels like to be sold to by someone else in your marketplace. Use what you learn to adapt your pitch.

- **Say you understand** – you ask open and closed questions to understand the customer's situation and need. But saying to them 'I understand because …' will build the trust between you. (Don't bore them, though, with your own product experiences.)

- **Show you agree** – customer enquiries are often prompted by some experience or event. If that was a bad experience (perhaps something broke), sympathize with their frustration or anger.

- **Say if you disagree** – but explain that you fully understand and respect the customer's stance.

- **Listen to your inner voice** – and ask sensitive questions when you sense there is something important your customer needs encouragement to say. This is really important if you are selling to people at a time of stress (e.g. arranging a funeral).

Finally, you need to show that you care and genuinely want to help your customer make good decisions. But equally important is not to cross the line and take the customer's side to the detriment of your firm. It can be surprisingly easy to 'go native' when selling.

'THE OPPOSITE OF ANGER IS NOT CALMNESS, IT'S EMPATHY.'

MEHMET ÖZ

! Good selling

… is being able to share your customer's feelings without losing your objectivity and focus.

Developing your style

Your selling style needs to be appropriate for your customer group, marketplace and the culture of your organization. It must also work for you so must reflect your own age, experience and personality. You need not only to relate to your customer but to feel comfortable yourself. You will not come over as sincere unless genuinely being yourself.

We've all received those scripted cold phone calls from overseas call centres where the person making the call is clearly reading from a script. What's worse is that they ask a lot of closed questions then use screen prompts to tell them what to say (or read) next.

As a rule, you will be more effective as a salesperson if you are:

• open and share information freely with your customer, rather than try to hold stuff back

• tolerant of differences of customer opinion, taste and perception

• willing to listen as well as to tell

• genuine and honest, with the confidence to say it 'like it is'.

It may also help you to develop a memorable style of dress. While you don't want to be too outlandish, it can help to have something by way of a visual trade mark. For example, you might always wear red shoes, wear a distinctive brooch, or, if you are a man, have a waxed moustache.

A distinctive look will help you if you sell, particularly if you sell at exhibitions or in a showroom. People you've spoken to once will come back to you personally if you are easy to remember. It's also true to say that, even if it's some while since a prospective customer visited you, they will expect you to remember them. As well as making yourself easy to spot, you need to be good at recognizing and remembering others.

Clearly, each sales interview will need you to vary your style. For example, a young hipster will expect quite a different style of sales meeting from an 80-year-old grandmother. However, you cannot assume that the hipster will expect to be called by their first name, nor that the old lady will expect you to be formal. You have to pay attention to each prospect's style and make an effort to mirror it.

Mirroring is something we do instinctively. If I smile, you smile. If you yawn, I yawn. And if you scratch your ear, I will probably scratch mine soon, too. As a salesperson, you want to mirror your prospect's body language and repeat some of their words. That's because it shows you are both attentive and in tune.

Don't become too self-conscious about your style or mirroring your prospect. Just be aware that it's important and allow your instinct to guide you.

Selling to couples

As with presenting to groups (covered in Chapter 10 in the section headed 'Interview panels), you need to make sure you engage both partners. If you focus solely on one, you will unwittingly alienate the other.

If the couple are a long-established 'item', you also need to watch their body language carefully. The non-verbal communication between them will be subtle, but significant. It's likely that they will check with each other in this way before making any commitment, even if it's just to consider the proposition you are making.

Here are some tips to help you sell successfully to couples:

- Keep both in view – arrange the seating so they sit side by side, facing you. It means that you can see both at the same time and, more importantly, notice when they look at each other.

- Make sure that both have time for the meeting – if one has to leave, or becomes distracted by, for example, a child, your opportunity to sell will be delayed, if not lost.

- Take a break – if selling in someone's home and one partner has to go out of the room, suggest you both wait until she or he returns. If they don't, encourage the remaining partner to bring them back.

- Summarize frequently – people pick up information at different speeds. Stopping to summarize will make sure that both keep up. It will also prompt the quieter of the two to ask questions.

- Use the toilet – sometimes it's obvious when a couple want to discuss the proposal without you present. This is your cue to go to the toilet, even if you don't need to.

- It's also very important to use open and closed questions to keep the meeting moving. The more people there are in a meeting, the longer it can take. You need to manage your time and not waste that of your prospect. Keep the meeting moving.

> **! Good selling**
>
> Control the pace of a sales meeting by asking questions that will help you identify the barriers to a sale. This keeps things on track and demonstrates that you are professional.

Getting the sale

The best sales interviews feel like a conversation. You use the techniques and tips in this book to direct and lead the prospect towards commitment. But this should not be obvious, other than that you are taking the lead. This changes when the time comes to close the deal. When you see the signs that the customer is ready (remember the 'buying signals' covered in Chapter 4), you need to ask for the order.

Closing was also introduced in Chapter 4, but now it's time to go into the subject in a little more detail. Closing is the most important part of the selling process. That's not just because it can get you the commitment you seek. It's also important because asking for the order prompts your prospect to tell you why they're not ready yet.

Close too little and your prospect, if ready to buy, will quickly become bored and frustrated. In fact, you can lose a sale by not asking for it. Close too frequently and your prospect will usually, if feeling pressured, tell you so. Then you can back off and take things a little more gently.

The best salespeople close the deal almost without the prospect noticing. They simply draw the interview to a close and thank the prospect for the order. The deal is done almost without the prospect feeling pressed at all.

My guess is that you're not quite that experienced yet. Before introducing some proven closing techniques, let's deal with the reason some salespeople fear closing. Too often they hang back from asking for commitment because they:

• fear rejection and feel uncomfortable when the prospect says 'no'
• worry that they will appear too pushy or desperate and might upset or offend the prospect

- don't feel confident they can handle the objections they feel attempting to close will prompt.

Conquering each of these quite understandable and commonly held fears is important. Overcoming them will remove any inhibitions you may have. Even picking up the telephone to make cold calls will lose its terror! Here are the three golden rules of selling:

1 **Don't take rejection personally** – when a customer says 'no', they are rejecting the proposition, not rejecting you. Recognize and remember this.

2 **If you push too hard, the prospect will simply push back** – it's human nature for someone to say when you're making them feel uncomfortable, but not when you're making them feel too comfortable. Accept the need to be assertive, then stay just the right side of the line.

3 **Never worry that you won't know the answer** – the most important thing is identifying the question.

When confronted by a question you can't answer, there are three ways to deal with it:

1 Ask the prospect if they know the answer, because then they will give you some context to the question and together you can usually work out the answer.

2 Check online and ring your office for help. Nobody expects you to know all the answers, just where to look to find them.

3 Ignore it and carry on if you feel it is insincere or a frivolous attempt to put you off.

> 'I TAKE REJECTION AS SOMEONE BLOWING A BUGLE IN MY EAR TO WAKE ME UP AND GET GOING, RATHER THAN RETREAT.'
>
> SYLVESTER STALLONE

! Good selling

Remember the ABC of selling – Always Be Closing.

Closing techniques

There are many techniques I use to gain commitment and close a sale. All are really little more than common sense and you should find them all easy to use. The art of closing is not to make a big deal of it, or change the pace and tempo of the meeting. Just use one of these techniques to close the deal or identify the objections you have yet to overcome. (This is called 'trial closing'.)

Here, then, is a list of closing techniques with a brief explanation of each:

- **Alternative close** – you provide two options, one of which is very specific and the other less so. Whichever is chosen means the order is placed. To say 'no' requires effort because that wasn't one of the options offered:

  'Would you like to arrange delivery for Thursday afternoon or one day next week?'

- **Assumptive close** – the prospect is dithering a little. You know you have answered all the questions and they're just hesitant about saying 'yes'. So you say 'yes' for them:

  'So I'll place the order with the factory and you can expect delivery next week sometime. Is there anything else you'd like to buy today?'

- **Bracket close** – you offer three options, with the one you expect them to buy in the middle. Often, the highest-priced option – usually far more expensive – is rarely booked and mostly there to make the others appear better value:

  'So we have available a basic room at £80, a deluxe room at £100 or a luxury suite at £150. Which shall I book for you?'

- **Bonus close** – you throw in some extras in exchange for commitment right now:

  'I tell you what, if you give the order now for the GLS model, I'll throw in free floor mats and the tow bar you need.'

- **Calculator close** – you literally work out the final price having listed all the variables (ideally on a printed order form) with the customer. You then write in the total and pass over the form with a pen for them to sign:

  'Right, so you need 20 tonnes at £100 per tonne, plus an applicator at £250, delivery at £100 and insurance at £50, that comes to £2,400; could you sign just here, please?'

- **Conditional close** – there's one often difficult objection remaining to overcome. You ask whether you can have the order if you can solve the problem:

  'So if I can find a way to get these packed in 10s rather than 20s, we have a deal? Let me ring the warehouse and see what we can do.'

- **Reversal close** – place the product on the table and then ignore it while you sell what you're there to discuss. Then, at the end, put it back in your bag. The customer will then ask what it was. You say:

  'Oh, we sell those to our bigger customers, I'm not sure you'd find the extra efficiency it delivers worth the price it costs.' (This, of course, ignites the customer's interest and they buy one.)

- **Ownership close** – this works well with cars and other tangible products the prospect physically tries out. Smaller products you can unpack and, once they've tried it, you just don't put it back in the box:

  'Wow, you've really got the hang of using yours; it took me a while to get the hang of it. I need to go now, so we just need to sort out payment?'

- **Ultimatum close** – highlight the downside of not making the purchase:

  'You do know that your insurance may be invalidated if you have a fire and no smoke detector?'

Can you see how each can be woven into your sales conversation? Closing is not a big deal, unless you make it a big deal!

Objections

Because you are now going to do more trial closing, you are going to unearth objections more frequently. You are also going to close more sales. Let's take a closer look at objections.

There are two kind of objection raised in response to a trial close:

- **Sincere objections** – these are where the prospect is not yet convinced, or needs to know in more detail how the features and benefits apply in their situation. These are easily dealt with because you simply need to reassure or resolve the concern.

- **Insincere objections** – these are far harder to deal with because they do not reveal the true reason the prospect is not prepared to commit. The prospect is not willing to reveal the true reason for not buying so throws spurious reasons at you to put you off the scent.

You can usually spot insincere objections because they do not logically fit within the conversation you are having. When handling sincere objections, you will find they will naturally be focused around a general area of concern. Insincere objections are often raised randomly, with no logic as to why they're raised when they are.

Insincere objections are commonly raised when:

- the person doesn't want to admit that they lack the authority to make the decision
- they want it, but can't afford it
- the order is usually yours but they gave it to a rival and are too embarrassed to admit it.

If faced with insincere objections, you will not get anywhere unless you confront your suspicion. Say something like, 'I don't think you're being straight with me here – is there something you're not telling me?' This is a little direct, but the alternative is to continue the conversation with no hope of commitment.

'AN OBJECTION IS NOT A REJECTION; IT IS SIMPLY A REQUEST FOR MORE INFORMATION.'

BO BENNETT

! Good selling

If you don't think your prospect is being straight with you, ask them – don't just plough on regardless. Your intuition, if trusted, will rarely let you down.

In this chapter you've discovered:

- that it's important to connect emotionally with your customer
- that your individuality is an asset not a handicap
- that closing is not a big deal, more something you gently do at every opportunity.

18.
Negotiation – the give and take of sales

Win–win

When you walk into a convenience store to buy some chocolate, the transaction is simple and straightforward. You pick a bar of your favourite brand off the shelf, take it to the checkout and pay the price asked. When you go out to buy a house, the asking price is just the starting point for a process of negotiation.

In a negotiation, both sides come to understand each other's priorities and needs. There's give and take on both sides so that, when the deal is finally struck, everyone is happy. You will find that most successful salespeople are actually very effective negotiators.

Negotiation almost inevitably involves compromise. It is defined as a 'process by which people settle differences'. If you stick to your guns and refuse to negotiate, the result is often argument and always disappointment. So, instead, you use your selling skills to reach an agreement that works for you both. That's not always possible but, more often than not, a realistic agreement is reached.

To negotiate, you need knowledge. You have to understand the true cost of what you are selling so that you do not find yourself selling at a loss. You also need an appreciation of your customer's situation, so that you know the value of your product or service to them.

Finally, negotiation is very different from haggling. It's not a matter of just pushing the price down or the specification up. It's about both sides making concessions to reach what is often a very pragmatic solution.

Selling	Negotiating
Wins orders	Wins contracts
Short-term gain	Long-term gain

'LET US NEVER NEGOTIATE OUT OF FEAR. BUT LET US NEVER FEAR TO NEGOTIATE.'

JOHN F. KENNEDY

Trading concessions

One of my first sales jobs was with a company that manufactured agricultural fertilizers. The factory on Humberside produced more than a million tonnes of products in a year. Farmers mostly use fertilizer in the spring and early summer when crops are growing. So the company faced two very real challenges: first, where to stockpile products produced 'out of season' and, second, how to fund the business if all the sales take place in the first third of the year.

Stockpiling used to involve transporting products out to warehouses around the country. This was costly and often meant that, when the season arrived, stock was in the wrong part of the country and had to be shipped again. Sales forecasting could never be totally accurate as, of course, what farmers choose to grow each year dictates the fertilizer products they need. This all added cost and reduced profits.

Farmers, on the other hand, usually have plenty of storage space. Grain harvested in the summer is usually sold by midwinter, giving them room to take next spring's fertilizer over the winter. To encourage farmers to buy and take their fertilizer out of season, the price list was discounted so that the further ahead it was purchased, the lower the price.

Let's look at how both sides benefit from this arrangement:

Farmers	Fertilizer company
Pay less for fertilizer bought out of season	Cash flow all year round
Take delivery early, using otherwise empty space	Products moved only once, from factory to farm, saving storage and re-delivery cost
Know that they have the product when they need it	Knows it's in the right place

Perhaps the biggest benefit to me as a salesman was that I did not have to try to talk to all of my customers at once. Instead, I sold them the bulk of their spring requirement over the autumn and winter. An added bonus was that, when they found they needed a few tonnes more in the spring, they'd inevitably buy the same brand they had stored in their sheds. That meant extra 'top-up' orders for me.

The benefits each side gains from this arrangement are called 'concessions'. Ideally, a concession has a greater value to the recipient than its cost to you. In the example above:

- the discounted price the farmers paid gave a better return than leaving their money in the bank
- the discount the company gave, plus the saving in storage costs, saved it money, too.

In this example, both sides gain because it costs the farmers nothing to store fertilizer in their barns, but it does cost the company to store its products.

Other examples of negotiations include:

- the discount you are offered to take shop-soiled goods
- the premium you pay for just-in-time delivery to reduce your investment in held stock
- the conservatory salesman who 'throws in' free blinds if you place the order today.

Can you see how important it is to fully understand both your own and your customer's situation before you start to negotiate? It's the reason you will almost always get the best deal from the boss of a small business rather than from one of the sales team.

❗ Negotiate well

Give away the things that cost you little but have great value to your customer.

Preparation

Some negotiations take years to finalize. For example, the deals airlines strike with aircraft manufacturers are large and complex. The airline needs to keep its operating costs low and the manufacturer has substantial development and overhead costs to cover.

You can bet that, when both sides sit down to negotiate, everyone involved will have done a lot of very careful preparation. Only by fully understanding the cost base of each other's business, plus having researched what's happening in their respective marketplaces, can they negotiate a deal than enables both to make money.

Sometimes, external factors have to be taken into account. For example, there may be government subsidies and grants to save jobs that could be lost if the deal falls through.

Here are some things you can do to prepare for a negotiation with a prospective long-term customer:

- Know your own costs and what you can concede easily and what you cannot.
- Research your prospect's situation to understand what about your product or service is most important to them.
- Know your competitors and the likely value to your prospect of any significant points of difference.
- What are the industry norms you might be asked to comply with.
- You need to go into the meeting with as much of the information you feel you may need as possible. You also need to recognize that your potential customer will have done their homework on you, too!

'BY FAILING TO PREPARE, YOU ARE PREPARING TO FAIL.'

BENJAMIN FRANKLIN

! **Negotiate well**

Negotiating is like taking an exam: you need to be well prepared, confident and rested when you walk into the room.

Stay objective

Fifteen years ago I bought a derelict farmstead and converted the main barn into our family home. When I was negotiating the deal, I thought I had found something unique and was understandably anxious to take possession. My enthusiasm to buy probably weakened my negotiating stance. The seller knew I was enthusiastic to buy and so had to concede little.

Once I started converting the barn, I started noticing others. In fact, my part of the country is littered with old brick barns, all now too small for modern farming practices. Although very content with my home, I'm pretty sure that, with the benefit of hindsight, I could have found another quite easily if I had been unable to buy the one I now own.

Had I entered into negotiation with two or three farmers, all with barns that met my needs, I could have negotiated a far more advantageous deal, particularly so if each had known I was also in talks with others.

In reality, there are few unique opportunities, although that can appear to be the case because:

- emotional attachment to a potential purchase can make the buyer blind to alternatives
- the desire to sell to the customer in your hand can make you oblivious to those waiting in the bush
- the more you focus on one deal, the harder it becomes to remain aware of alternatives.

You will always negotiate more successfully if the other person knows you are prepared to walk away from the deal. Equally, when you are the salesperson, you have to do all you can to illustrate how your offer is unique.

> 'A WISE MAN SHOULD HAVE MONEY IN HIS HEAD, BUT NOT IN HIS HEART.'
>
> JONATHAN SWIFT

! Negotiate well

You negotiate with your head and a calculator, not your heart and a handkerchief.

How to negotiate

Negotiation comes at the very end of the sales process. You've converted interest to desire, and your prospect is now convinced they can benefit from what it is you are selling. However, as you try to close the deal, it becomes apparent that it's not as simple as getting a straightforward 'yes'.

It could be that the specification or the terms under which you will do business together need to be a little different. However, the potential business that will result if you reach agreement means that it's worth the effort to negotiate a little.

So the first key point is this: you only start negotiating when the deal has been agreed in principle. You negotiate on the how, where and when, rather than on the what, why or if. At a very practical level, you can think of a negotiation as selling the details when the rest of the deal has been agreed.

As such, a negotiation is just like a sales interview. You use open and closed questions; you quantify benefits; and you should 'always be closing'. The difference is in the level of detail. So, when you are negotiating, remember the following:

- **Write things down** – list the key points on a piece of paper and add each concession as it is agreed. Also, write down any calculations so that you have a record of what you've agreed and how the figures were arrived at.

- **Trade don't give** – for every point you concede, your prospect must also concede a point. You agree to free delivery and in return she agrees to pay within 7 rather than 31 days. Each concession you make should be conditional on the concession your buyer makes in return.

- **Prioritize** – if you negotiate the main sticking points first, the secondary ones will, when you reach them, appear far less important and probably be very quickly agreed.

- **Take your time** – even if the concession is one you can easily make, take your time to consider it before agreeing. You want your buyer to feel that they are pushing you hard, even when they are not.

- **Be flexible** – if you concede a few very minor points easily, your buyer will feel compelled to reciprocate. What they concede in return might well have value to you.

- **Listen carefully** – when negotiating, you have to listen even harder for those hidden clues. Always read between the lines and try to work out what concerns or issues might be behind the words you are hearing.

- **Summarize often** – it helps you both to stay focused if you summarize the deal so far after each concession trade has taken place. Also, use the opportunity to trial close. You might have gone far enough to agree the deal.

- **Sign the notes** – this is a personal preference of mine. Having written down each point and any calculations along the way, once the deal is done, I will sign the notes and ask the customer to do the same. Then I'll send a copy to the customer when I confirm the order later. This reminds both parties what's been agreed. More importantly, it makes it far harder for anyone to challenge the agreement later and try to change the deal – your buyer's boss, for example.

Remember that, when you negotiate with someone, you have already agreed in principle to do business together. Your negotiation should therefore be friendly and collaborative. You may be taking the lead, but you are working together to find a solution.

> 'UNLESS BOTH SIDES WIN, NO AGREEMENT CAN BE PERMANENT.'
>
> JIMMY CARTER

! Negotiate well

You negotiate over the icing when you have already agreed to buy the cake.

Getting paid

If you sell as part of your job, you will at some time inevitably find yourself responsible for collecting the money. Getting paid often requires careful negotiation and, contrary to common belief, pursuing unpaid debts through the court system is no guarantee of success, even if you win judgment.

In fact, on my first day in one new sales job I was asked to visit a customer to collect a cheque. This was before it was possible to make online payments and a postal strike meant that the customer could not mail the cheque. I phoned to say that I'd be popping in on my way home (I lived near his office) and turned up at the appointed time.

He regaled me with a catalogue of reasons why he should not be making this payment. There were, he said, problems with the product, problems with the after-sales service, and my new boss was obsessed with money. This was all very unsettling on my first day, but I sat it out until he finally stopped complaining. At last, he took out his chequebook and gave me the payment I'd gone to collect.

This actually was quite easy. I've also knocked on people's doors late at night to ask for money, been threatened with a shotgun, and introduced one near-bankrupt client to a mortgage broker able to refinance his house so that he could pay me.

I share these anecdotes not to impress but to make the point that, however scary collecting unpaid debts might seem, in reality it's fairly straightforward. Even the man with the gun was really only posturing and eventually wrote me a cheque.

Here, then, are some points to help you negotiate when your job includes making sure that your company gets paid:

- **Keep them trading** – if you stop someone trading, they lose the ability to pay you at all. It's better to accept stage or delayed payments to enable them to trade their way out of debt.

- **Stay friendly** – it's lonely getting into debt and, if you are the creditor who's most helpful (without being a pushover), you're more likely to get paid before people who shout and threaten.

- **Help them remove the cause** – sometimes your customer needs help using your product more profitably. Be prepared to offer some free consultancy. It's worth it because, once back in the black, they will become one of your most loyal supporters.

Handling complaints

Another test of your negotiation skills comes when your customer complains. It might well be that they have encountered a problem and have good reason to be unhappy. Handled well, a complaint can build trust and your customer's commitment to you. Handled badly, it can fester and damage your reputation. Here's a checklist to help you handle complaints effectively:

- **Sympathize** – but don't admit liability. Don't take any anger as a personal attack on you. Remain polite and calm, and take notes.
- **Listen** – and summarize back to the customer the key points to gain agreement. Agreeing what the problem is takes you one step closer to solving it.
- **Stay positive** – be upbeat and try to help the customer see their issue in context.
- **Find facts** – often, when people are angry or upset, they assume that you have the facts already. Get them to spell out exactly what happened. Often, this process helps you identify a misunderstanding.
- **Agree to help** – you can promise to investigate and get back to the customer within an agreed timescale. Commit to what you can realistically do, again without admitting liability.
- **Trade concessions** – sometimes, even if the complaint turns out not to be your firm's fault, it can be worth doing something to solve it. When you do this, have the customer agree to do something for you in return, for example place an additional order.

Most salespeople will say that some of their best customers stay with them because of the way they handled a complaint.

'NOTHING TRAVELS FASTER THAN THE SPEED OF LIGHT WITH THE POSSIBLE EXCEPTION OF BAD NEWS, WHICH OBEYS ITS OWN SPECIAL LAWS.'

DOUGLAS ADAMS

! Negotiate well

Negotiate your way out of problems with the same enthusiasm you negotiate your way into new business.

In this chapter you've discovered:

- that once you've sold the principle, you negotiate on the detail
- that you trade concessions, rather than give them away
- that negotiation skills can help you solve problems as well as win customers.

19.

Exhibitions – how to succeed at shows

Your big event

Exhibitions come in all shapes and sizes – from a small business-to-business event in your home city to a major business-to-consumer show such as London's 'Ideal Home'. Attending an exhibition concentrates the sales process, compresses it, and forces you to think and act quickly.

Visitors to your stand also have the opportunity to visit your competitors, who may be standing just a few metres away. They can also come in droves, forcing you to choose whom to speak to and whom to let go. And, strangely, especially at shows attended by the general public, you can find yourself asked the same question with such regularity that you can almost answer it before it is asked.

Yet an exhibition represents a large investment for any organization. Time, planning and attending, hotels, food, impressive displays, printed literature and pre-event advertising can all add up to a significant sum. Attending trade shows and public exhibitions can be your best opportunity for face-to-face contact with your target audience.

Not only do you have the opportunity to sell to people you would otherwise never meet, but you can conduct market research, too. Visitors will soon tell you what they do or don't like about what you have on display. If you sell a product people can use, you have the added benefit of seeing people pick it up and try it for the first time.

Rather like advertising, there will be no shortage of people trying to sell your organization a stand at an exhibition. If you are involved in choosing whether or not to attend, here are some questions to ask yourself before making the decision:

- How well does the event target your marketplace?
- Has the organizer delivered a similar successful event before?
- What opportunities will there be for your firm to feature in pre-event promotion?

- Are you being offered a stand where everyone will pass, or at the end of a blind alley?
- What else is happening at the same time that could boost or reduce attendance?

Don't be swayed by the opportunity to 'raise your profile', attend just because a competitor is, or because you fear missing out. Be objective and invest time and money in an exhibition only when you are confident it will deliver you value for money.

> 'THE INTELLIGENCE OF THE CREATURE KNOWN AS A CROWD IS THE SQUARE ROOT OF THE NUMBER OF PEOPLE IN IT.'
>
> TERRY PRATCHETT

> **! Exhibition success**
>
> An exhibition is only an opportunity if you make it an opportunity. It's all in the planning.

Planning

The reasons you attend an exhibition are to win new customers and to influence people. It is important to set realistic targets for both of these. Only when you know what you want to achieve from an exhibition can you plan to succeed. For example, you might want to:

- sell existing products and services
- test market a new product and gauge visitors' reaction to it
- strengthen your relationship with existing customers
- support distributors of your products by being a technical expert on their stand
- meet industry opinion formers who you know will be visiting the event.

Most firms attending an exhibition will want to do all of these things to a greater or lesser extent. Trying to do everything within the confines of a three-by-two-metre space, however, is difficult. Indeed, if you have any influence over the design and layout of your stand, encourage colleagues to remember that 'less can deliver more'. All exhibition stands should be simple and:

- make it obvious what you are selling at first glance to anyone walking by
- have a single, simple, benefit-led theme
- offer visitors some incentive to stop and talk, perhaps a competition, survey or special exhibition deal.

If you know the people you want to visit your stand, perhaps existing customers and prospects you've identified, send them a personal invitation and maybe even follow this up by phone. Offer an incentive to attend, for example:

- the opportunity to preview your next-generation machine
- an early-morning reception, to encourage key people to come to you first
- the opportunity to win a prize – ideally, of the 'bring this with you to qualify' kind.

If your target audience is fairly small, you will need to work harder to get them to your stand. Try posting a key to each prospect, along with a picture of the locked box you will have on your stand. Only one key opens the box and releases the prize. Keys and other physical objects will always be more effective than printed invitations.

Don't forget to make good use of social media to attract visitors. Use them both to prompt debate and bring people to your stand. You can:

- use a specific hashtag (#youroffer) to encourage people to visit
- distribute a QR code that can be scanned on your stand in return for a reward
- link visiting your stand to raising money for charity.

Finally, don't forget to hold a pre-exhibition briefing for all attending. You want to make sure that everyone:

- understands the objectives for the event
- is familiar with any show offers or deals
- knows when they should be on the stand and when they should be checking out the competition.

Remember, too, that an exhibition is a great opportunity to polish your sales technique. You will carry out many short sales interviews. Reflect on each and see how you can develop your technique over the course of the event.

> SUCCESS DEPENDS UPON PREVIOUS PREPARATION, AND WITHOUT SUCH PREPARATION THERE IS SURE TO BE FAILURE.
>
> CONFUCIUS

! **Exhibition success**

Encourage colleagues to mystery-shop competing exhibition stands and be aware that competitors will be mystery-shopping yours.

Being approachable

I can remember one exhibition I attended where, at lunchtime, the organizer placed his foil-wrapped homemade sandwiches and flask of coffee on the registration desk. He continued signing people in as he munched. He had no idea that this was unprofessional and off-putting for visitors. I'm sure that you would not do anything like this, but let's start with a few tips on how to present yourself at an exhibition:

- **Stand, don't sit** – this enables you to make eye contact with passers-by and invite them to your stand.
- **Stand out** – it can be difficult at a busy event to tell who's manning the stand. Consider wearing branded T-shirts, or, if a more formal event, branded hats.
- **Sleep well** – the bar can be a very real distraction for some when staying in a hotel with colleagues. Early nights are better for exhibitions; save the party until the end.
- **Smile** – this can become progressively harder as you tire, but you do need to greet the fiftieth visitor with the same enthusiasm as you greeted the first.
- **Use teamwork** – play to your strengths. If you're uncomfortable pulling people off the aisles, have someone else do this and then pass them over to you. Consider hiring temps for this.

- **Stay to the end** – often the best deals are done while your rivals are packing up their stands to go home.
- **Never assume** – you cannot judge a visitor by their appearance or even what is written on their badge. Treat everyone as a genuine prospect. Remember the networking rules from Chapter 9 – whom can this person introduce you to?

Having enough people with you to arrange a proper rota is important. If you are working on your own, ask a friend to come along to give you some breaks. Brief them as best you can and have them take down contact details from the people they speak to. Ask them to tell people you will call them. Don't try to work an exhibition stand on your own all day.

> **! Exhibition success**
>
> Working an exhibition is like having 50 job interviews in a day: intense, inspiring and occasionally intimidating!

Selling

The doors have opened and visitors are streaming into the exhibition hall. You are ready, briefed, fresh and eager to do business. How are you actually standing right now? The chances are you have your arms folded. It's probably unintentional, but, for most of us, especially men, it's the most comfortable way to stand. It is also negative, uninviting body language, creating a barrier between you and those who might approach your stand.

Breaking the ice

It actually takes some courage to walk off the aisle and on to an exhibition stand. As a visitor, you are almost inevitably going to be approached and, if only casually interested, will quickly feel embarrassed if cornered by a pushy salesperson. You certainly don't want someone creeping up behind you and saying, 'How can I help you?'

So, when you are on the stand, watching the flow of people walking past, seek eye contact and, when you make it, smile. Perhaps point to the key feature on your stand, perhaps a piece of equipment, rolling video display or literature rack. Do not simply hand out leaflets to everyone going past. You want people to stop and talk.

Next, you need to engage the visitor in conversation. You should lead with an open question. This is less threatening and will help you establish rapport. You might develop a few ice-breaking open questions to use. Here are some that work for me:

- 'I've not been outside for ages – what's the weather doing?'
- 'What do you think of ...? (Point to something on your stand.)
- 'What brings you to the show today?'

Each is intended to do no more than stop the passer by and open dialogue.

Qualifying the visitor

So much depends on what you are selling and the nature of the event. If you're selling artisan cheeses at a food fair, everyone you talk to has the potential to buy. If, however, you are selling machine tools at an engineering expo, only a small proportion of visitors may be in the market for your products.

That makes it really important that you qualify your visitor as quickly as possible. This is because, unlike a sales visit, you may be ignoring a genuine prospect while in conversation with someone who has no intention or ability to buy. They could be a student, selling something themselves, or just one of those random people you always encounter milling around at an exhibition. For some attendees, even a trade show is just a day out!

So, having engaged the person in conversation, you need to quickly turn the conversation round to the reason you are there. Use open and closed questions to determine:

- what has prompted their interest in your products/services and stand
- whether they are in the market right now, and, if not, when
- whether they can afford to buy what you are selling (beware, as appearances can be deceptive)
- whether they are the decision maker and, if not, how you and they can influence the buying decision.

You can probably do this more assertively at a business-to-business event than at one attended by members of the public. At a busy show, you need to qualify people quickly and efficiently. Many, if not immediately in the market, will be happy to browse on their own once you have spoken with them. Most will understand that you need to focus on those with a more pressing need to discuss your offer.

It is always important to record the names and contact details of those you meet at an exhibition. In some markets, there can be a very long lead time from enquiry to order (for example, buying a second home or replacement trucks).

If you find that the person is not really in the market for what you do, you have three options:

1 Find out whether they have the potential to introduce you to someone who can buy from you.

2 Chat with them because a busy stand is more likely to attract a visitor than an empty one.

3 Politely move them on so that you can focus on the other people heading your way.

You can then focus on spending a few minutes with each of the people you meet through the day who offer the greatest potential. If you are selling consumer products to the public, it should be straightforward. You go through the sales process quickly and efficiently.

However, if you operate in a business-to-business environment, particularly if selling capital equipment or other high-value products or services, you may need to be more selective and spend more time with fewer prospects.

Larger exhibition stands often have a private room where these conversations can take place. If you don't have that luxury, have somewhere you can take people for a quiet coffee. This can be difficult within an exhibition hall, but often there's somewhere suitable outside, usually within five minutes' walk. Check this out before the show so that you know you have somewhere to go.

Closing

Closing well is really important at an exhibition. If you leave a prospect interested but not committed, they may well complete the purchase on the next stand they visit. Even if yours is not a product or service people can buy and take away with them, you need to commit them to something tangible.

Ideally, you need commitment to something that will be difficult for the prospect to ignore easily. You need to make them 'sticky' – that is, reduce the likelihood of them going elsewhere.

For example, you could arrange a date in both of your diaries to meet during the week after the exhibition. This makes it less likely that the order will be placed elsewhere at the exhibition. The prospect would find ringing you to cancel the meeting embarrassing.

Other ways to make your prospects 'sticky' and safe from competitors include the following:

- giving them a sample to take away that you need to pick up when you come to visit them
- keeping something belonging to customers until after the show – even offering to store their coat behind your stand for the day will help
- promising to check some facts out, or producing an estimate for them during the day and arranging a time near the close of the event for them to return to meet you.

In each case, use the closing techniques suggested in this book to gain commitment. Remember, you need to close as each milestone is reached. Closing well reassures your prospect and creates a firm foundation for the next meeting. Then you can quickly recap and move on closer to the sale.

'CHOOSE PEOPLE WHO LIFT YOU UP.'

MICHELLE OBAMA

! Exhibition success

You won't have time to talk to everyone, so make sure that you ask everyone whether they are the best person for you to talk to right now.

Following up

I have attended and worked at many exhibitions and, after each one, I find at least one business card I cannot remember collecting. It's usually from someone in a senior role who appears to be a good prospect, but what we talked about has completely been forgotten. It is very, very easy to take a card, agree to some action, then pocket the card and start talking to the next person waiting for you on the stand.

Equally, I have visited exhibitions, been excited by something I've seen, enquired, left my details and heard nothing more from the firm. I rarely pick up the phone to remind them. My concern (and perhaps your concern, too) is that, if they lose a sales lead, they may well fall short in other ways, too. I usually buy elsewhere.

When you follow up with people after an exhibition, they will expect you to remember:

- who they are and the gist of what they told you
- what it was they were most interested in
- the action you both agreed would take place after the exhibition.

The way to do this is to take good notes as you speak with each prospect on the stand. You can do this using a tablet computer, but it's often easier to use a more traditional pen and notepad. Then you can staple the prospect's business card to the page.

You can then scan and send each page back to your office in a quiet moment, attached to an email that lists the actions you've promised. This can enable your prospect to receive a follow-up email answering any urgent queries before they leave the exhibition. You can also invite them back at the end. Use technology to support your selling, but never become reliant on it. Batteries always seem to run down faster at an exhibition than anywhere else you go.

The day after the exhibition, make a point of following up each lead individually. The longer you leave a lead before following it up, the lower your chances of converting it into a sale.

Sometimes, particularly if you've used competition forms to collect contact details, you will have too many leads to follow up individually straight away. If this is likely, spend some time before the event putting together a follow-up email. Consider using a laptop rather than, say, those paper competition entry forms. Alternatively, collect business cards, scan them and import the data to a website from which you can send personalized emails to large numbers of people.

Finally, add a tick box to any competition entry form so that people consent to be followed up. It reminds them they will be followed up and reduces the chance of someone complaining later.

SUCCESS COMES FROM TAKING THE INITIATIVE AND FOLLOWING UP.

TONY ROBBINS

! Exhibition success

The notes you take at an exhibition are like cheques: each should carry the promise of future money in the bank.

Conferences

Attending a conference is in many ways similar to taking a stand at an exhibition. Indeed, many conferences have trade stands in the area where refreshments are served. If you are attending or exhibiting at a conference, you have additional sales opportunities you should not miss. These include:

- asking questions, which enables you to stand up and introduce yourself to the audience
- volunteering to speak, run workshops or chair sessions
- placing a printed 'delegate offer' on each seat in the conference hall or in the delegate packs
- commenting on the debate using social media and the conference hashtag to raise your profile and connect with other like-minded delegates
- organizing a fringe event to cover issues specific to your business sector.

It is relatively easy to get noticed at a conference if you do these things. In addition, I always make a point of:

- wearing bright clothes so I stand out from the sea of grey suits (men and women)
- sitting in the front row, making eye contact with keynote speakers and showing I appreciate the points they are making (this makes it easier to get some of their time during the breaks)
- tweeting positively, mentioning the organizers and key people in the room.

Lastly, to get the most from a conference, it pays to read around the key issues that will be addressed before you arrive. Have an opinion and perhaps a few prepared questions, too. Get involved!

'LET US WALK INTO THE CONFERENCE ROOM AS EQUALS AND NOT SECOND-CLASS CITIZENS.'

MARTIN MCGUINNESS

! **Conference success**

Be there, be noticed, be heard and be remembered!

In this chapter you've discovered:

- the importance of good preparation and planning
- that we all need to work at being approachable and therefore approached
- how important it is to take notes and follow up promptly.

20.
Selling more – boosting your performance

Food for thought

When did you last eat at a chain pizza restaurant? Think back to how they took your order. Once you were seated and settled with a menu, they'll have taken your drinks order. This is both hospitable but also good business practice. They know that, if you choose an alcoholic drink, you will be more likely to order more than if they take your food and drink order at the same time. And, obviously, the sooner you start drinking, the more likely you are to order more drinks later.

After writing down your drinks order, the waiter will almost inevitably ask whether you'd like some olives or bread with your drinks. You hadn't planned on ordering olives, but it seems a nice idea so you say 'yes'. The same thing happens when you order your main course; you have a side salad and extra topping. Then you are offered a desert and coffee.

While all of the extras can combine to convert a pleasant midweek meal out into a lavish treat, they also boost restaurant profitability. Just by asking, a good waiter can increase your spend by perhaps 50 per cent. That's a far more reliable way to boost the evening's income than hoping that another couple will arrive to take your table after you've left.

This process is called 'upselling'. It's just one of the easier ways you can sell to more existing customers.

It makes sense to sell more to existing customers for a number of reasons, not all of them obvious. Here are some you might not have considered:

• They already buy from you and so understand much of what you do.

• You know that they will pay with more certainty than if you'd never dealt with them before.

• You may already be making regular deliveries to them, so the on-costs are low.

It can help to look at each customer you have and calculate their profitability. Total the cost of the time you spend keeping in touch, together with administrative and delivery costs. Then look at the value of the current annual spend with you. Now take one from the other to calculate their net value. For example, let's assume you sell bed linen to a hotel:

• The hotel replaces its linen regularly and spends £20,000 a year with you.
• Your time meeting them quarterly and keeping in touch costs, say, £3,000 a year.
• Administration time processing invoices/payments plus delivery costs £2,000 a year.
• The contribution is therefore £15,000.

Next, assume that your firm starts selling clothing for chefs, waiting staff and cleaners. A hotel the size of your customer typically spends £5,000 per annum on uniforms. If you found a new hotel and supplied just uniforms and serviced them to the same extent as your existing customer, your costs and income would be equal. There would be no contribution and, as you have to buy the uniforms in, you would actually make a loss.

Taking your existing customer to a company launch of the new product range costs you £200 but the administration and delivery costs are unchanged as monthly deliveries and invoices now include both linen and uniforms. Now the uniforms are highly profitable because most of your costs of servicing the customer are already met.

So you can see the importance in both retail and business-to-business situations of selling more to the same customer.

'YOUR COMPANY'S MOST VALUABLE ASSET IS HOW IT IS KNOWN TO ITS CUSTOMERS.'

BRIAN TRACY

> ## ! Sell more
>
> It is almost always more profitable to sell new things to old customers than old things to new customers.

Upselling

This is where you increase the value of an order at the time it is placed. It can be surprisingly easy to upsell, yet many salespeople stop selling as soon as the first deal is agreed. Selling those profitable extras, or increasing the specification, is best done the moment the decision to buy has been reached. It's similar to asking for a referral. Always strike when the iron is at its hottest!

As well as the pizza restaurant example I used above, other examples of upselling include:

- encouraging someone booking a standard hotel room to pay the extra for a junior suite
- persuading someone ordering a car to add a servicing package to their monthly payment
- selling accidental damage/loss insurance when someone buys a new mobile phone.

When you close a sale, you have a very good idea of exactly what tipped the customer into making their purchase. Which of those SPACED buying motives (introduced in Chapter 4) are most important to this customer? Remember, each will be different. Here's an example.

Two people buy large, petrol-driven, ride-on lawnmowers. Stuart is 60 and a keen gardener with both formal lawns and an orchard. Felicity is a wealthy widow with a large country house. She has a gardener and, apart from managing the garden's budget, she goes outside only to cut flowers. Both buy identical mowers from you. But their motivations are quite different:

Buying motive	Stuart	Felicity
Safety	Drives himself so this is important	Assumes gardener can look after himself
Performance	Enjoys cutting grass so important, too	Important as wants fast work rate
Appearance	Likes showing off to neighbours	Functionality is everything – no interest
Convenience	Easy and a joy to drive	No intention of sitting on it
Durability	Will cherish and care for it	Has no intention of ever buying another

Now let's look at the list of extras you can offer Stuart and Felicity when they agree to buy their mowers:

Extra	Stuart	Felicity
Safety boots	Interested	No interest
Reverse as well as forward gears	Sees how it will boost performance	Worried about her herbaceous border, so yes, interested but for quite a different reason
Chrome trim	Loves the idea of lawnmower bling	Utterly ridiculous, she says
Deluxe seat	Had already checked this out online so 'yes please'	Believes 'staff' should welcome discomfort
Maintenance contract	Has no intention of letting anyone else near it with a spanner	Agrees it will help machine last longer, so 'yes'

Can you see how your knowledge of both buyers makes it easy to offer them the extras you think they're most likely to find interesting? What's more, the process of discussing how they will specifically benefit enables you to offer the extras easily. The art is to flow the upselling into the closing of the main deal.

Take a look back at the different closing techniques listed in Chapter 17. Some lend themselves particularly well to upselling. My favourite is a variation on the 'calculator' close. For the lawnmower example, it works like this:

- You fill in an order form for the mower, write down the model number and price, and seek agreement that this is what has just been agreed.
- Then, without moving your pen from the paper, you say:
  - 'You said you'll be driving this yourself, Stuart, and so I'd recommend we add the deluxe seat; it's only an additional £35 and you won't feel the bumps on rough grass in your orchard.'
  - 'You mentioned that your gardener is not the best mechanic, Felicity, so I'm guessing you'll want to add out annual maintenance and breakdown cover for £60 per annum.'
- As each extra is agreed, you add it to the order form and stop when you either run out of extras or, more likely, the customer says, 'That's enough.'

Because the upsold items are low-priced in relation to the price of the mower just agreed, it's really easy for the customer to agree to them. If, say, there was a four-week wait for the mower to arrive and you tried to add the extras when arranging delivery, this upselling technique would not work. You have to upsell at the moment the order is agreed.

Upselling works in just about every sales situation. What's most important is that, because you already have the customer, the profit margin on upsold items is always higher than if those items were sold separately. That's why using the 'bonus close' and negotiating a little can leave your customer buying more, yet also feeling they've had a great deal.

You use the bonus close to upsell by giving something with a high perceived value to the customer and low price to yourself. In return, they commit to something that boosts your profitability. For example, when buying a new car, you agree to upgrade to the higher-spec model in exchange for the dealer giving you free servicing for the first year. The higher spec earns the dealer more money than the likely cost of the one service the car will have in the first year. Furthermore, it can be agreed that the service is booked at short notice when the workshops are quiet.

> 'I SPEND HOURS MOWING THE LAWN IN ABSOLUTELY STRAIGHT LINES ON MY TRACTOR. IF IT'S NOT RIGHT, I DO IT AGAIN.'
>
> BRITT EKLAND

! Sell more

If you don't have opportunities to upsell to your customers, find some products and services you can add to create this opportunity to boost your profits.

Cross-selling

Cross-selling is where you sell new products to existing customers, or existing products to colleagues of current customers. The example earlier in this chapter illustrates how you can cross-sell. Selling staff uniforms to the hotel that already buys its linen from you boosts your income and profit. But, unless you tell the hotel manager that you now stock uniforms, she will not know.

Another example would be to gain an introduction to other hotels in the same group. Often, different units within the same organization buy individually. Each will have its own network of suppliers. While you might assume that a group of, say, hotel managers would share supplier information, often they do not. Remember that they may be competing to be the most profitable hotel in the group. You might be seen as part of that competitive advantage and so not automatically shared.

Customers very quickly come to know us for what we do for them. All suppliers get pigeonholed and you have to make a real effort to make your existing customers aware of new lines. You also have to keep in touch with changes to each existing customer's situation. These might create opportunities for you to sell things to them you mentioned years ago but they have forgotten you can provide.

The key to cross-selling is asking the right questions as often as you feel able. These include:

- 'Who else within your organization could benefit from this in the way you have?'
- 'What other businesses do you have that could use this?'
- 'Have I told you that we can now supply ...?'

And, of course, if you work within a group structure, do you have colleagues with whom you can swap customer introductions? We all tend to work in organizational silos, with too little shared knowledge or collaboration.

Here are some tips to prompt you to think about the cross-selling opportunities that you may be missing:

- Ask every customer you meet to tell you what's new in their world. This can help you spot opportunities. It also gives you the opportunity to reciprocate and tell them what's new with you.
- Put new things where people can see them. Think about how shops put the sweets next to the till. What are the equivalent ways you can place different products or services in front of your customers?
- Invite customers to product seminars and offer an incentive to bring a colleague who is yet to buy from you. Remember that new customers will judge you by the opinion of the colleague who invited them.

- Many websites now will offer you new products based on your purchase history. 'If you liked that, you'll probably like this.' Your customers may welcome intelligent introductions to new products or services that they've not tried but which experience tells you they will probably find useful.

- Offer incentives to try new products. Reward your existing customers with a discount on their first order of something they've not tried before. Conversely, offer them an incentive to introduce a colleague who becomes a customer, too.

- Bundle products and services so that existing customers have the opportunity to try new products they might otherwise not find interesting.

- Never underestimate the power of free. In other words, if you give people the chance to try a new product or service at no cost, most will inevitably try it. It's why supermarkets hand out samples of new food lines. Once people have tasted it, they are far more likely to buy. Furthermore, once they start buying, they will often continue. Purchasing behaviour is largely habitual.

'WE KEEP MOVING FORWARD, OPENING NEW DOORS, AND DOING NEW THINGS, BECAUSE WE'RE CURIOUS AND CURIOSITY KEEPS LEADING US DOWN NEW PATHS.'

WALT DISNEY

! Sell more

For your established customers, buying from you becomes a habit. Use this habit as a foundation, not a prop.

And finally

You will develop a more relaxed selling style as your confidence in your selling skills, knowledge of your products and services, and experience of handling the most common objections grow. This will enable you to ask much more searching questions of both your customers and prospects. Over time, you will discover that, if asked the right questions, your prospects and customers will nearly always help you find the right answers.

The key to boosting your sales is almost always effective communication. Of course, good marketing can raise awareness and prompt enquiries, but little can substitute for starting with your existing customers, and strengthening and building their commitment to you.

Let me reflect on my own selling success and share some of the things I believe have helped me to sell more:

- **Network** – I am pretty good at keeping in touch with people. Social media make this far simpler and I invest a lot of effort in keeping my 'loose ties' aware of what I do and what that means for those I work with. I send out a monthly e-newsletter (see www.robertashton.co.uk) and share it also with my LinkedIn network. But, most of all, I constantly invest in my network, offering help where I see it is needed, introducing people to each other and being positively proactive.

- **Opportunities** – I create lots of opportunities for people to benefit by helping me sell. For example, I've offered people and organizations within my network free places and financial incentives to populate the one-day course I've developed, based on this book. My connections are selling on my behalf. They find venue and delegates; I deliver the course. It's a win–win.

- **Evolution** – I constantly search for the trends that will help me adapt what I'm selling, for myself and others, to meet tomorrow's needs. Too many people moan about how their market has changed and left them behind. I strive to remain ahead of the curve.

- **Self-investment** – I make sure that I have all that I need to deliver peak sales performance. That includes using a personal trainer, decent technology, a new car every three years that's kept clean, and an able assistant, Chris, who does much of the groundwork for me.

- **Feedback** – I am naturally self-critical and so can find even constructive criticism difficult, but, without listening and responding to feedback, I would quickly find myself in a commercial cul de sac, missing market opportunity and wondering why.

As with all of my books, I invite you to share your selling challenges with me and I'll help if I can. I'd also love to hear how this book has helped you. We all enjoy learning how we've helped others.

You can reach me via my website www.robertashton.co.uk or follow me on Twitter @robertashton1

I look forward to hearing from you.

'INVEST THREE PERCENT OF YOUR INCOME IN YOURSELF (SELF-DEVELOPMENT) IN ORDER TO GUARANTEE YOUR FUTURE.'

BRIAN TRACY

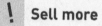 **Sell more**

My philosophy is simple: how can I expect others to invest in me if I don't invest in myself?

In this chapter you've discovered:

- that it's easier to sell new things to existing customers than anything to a new customer
- that, if you don't keep reminding people what you do, they won't know
- that I love reader feedback and hope we can stay in touch!

Index